THE BASICS OF....

MODEL GLIDERS

Chas Gardiner

NEXUS SPECIAL INTERESTS

Nexus Special Interests Ltd
Nexus House
Boundary Way
Hemel Hempstead
Herts HP2 7ST
England

First published 1995
© Chas Gardiner 1995

ISBN 1-85486-114-X

Design and typesetting by The Studio, Exeter
Printed and bound in Great Britain by Bell & Bain Ltd., Glasgow

Contents

Foreword

The childhood dream is to fly. If you don't know it yet, you will.

Flying is about mastery of the air and the elements, flying is about sport and transport, flying is about design for purpose, flying is about strength of materials, flying is about co-ordination of all these skills and the ability to become part of the entire machine.

Flying is about getting the most out of yourself.

Over successive generations, design and production engineers, pilots and crew, passengers and those who service aircraft all have one thing in common; a love of flight and flying. No one will tell you why, perhaps no one can tell you why. The aeroplane is the fulfilment of that childhood dream.

It is many years since one man could create an aeroplane from start to finish by himself. There are laws to ensure the safety of all who may be influenced by such work. This includes not only the people who might fly in that aircraft, but those that it might fall onto. With an aeroplane, every little detail must be right and nothing is left to chance. Thus we develop a philosophy that ensures that we get things right — first time.

One of the easiest axioms to remember is, *measure twice, cut once.*

Skills learned in anticipation and prevention of problems will influence your own life and you will be all the better for it.

As with all things manufactured, there must always be an element of care. A car is not dangerous in the showroom — drive it on the road and you are required by law to be able to pay compensation for any injury or damage it might cause while in your control. So it is with a model aircraft or any other device and a glider travelling out of control at speed can be painful.

Full size and model gliding have a lot in common.

There is insurance cover available at a modest cost, be sure that you are covered. Sources are contained within the appendix.

The hobby is all embracing including elements of aerodynamics, structures, strength of materials, engineering, innovation, draughtsmanship, computer applications, aesthetics, glass reinforced plastics, adhesives technology, flying skills, meteorology, logistics, patience, dedication, curiosity and not a little pride in one's achievements.

In addition to sport and industry, it may be worth mentioning the operation of remote controlled aircraft for military, monitoring and surveillance purposes. In a multi-million pound industry like that, few would admit to playing with toys.

Much of the design process is the same whether you are building a giant passenger carrying jet or a light aircraft but there is no way that a book this size is going to tell you all that. The skills that you would need to become any part of the team will be learned gradually and I believe that model flying is as good an introduction as you are going to get.

Of course, many people are pragmatists who do something because they know that it works for others and should work for them. Invariably it does.

Since you are keen to learn, let's start with gliding. This aspect of flight does not use an engine, just the powers of gravity and air movement and as such is perhaps more demanding on design and flying skills than any other. Certainly, the average glider pilot knows more about his craft than his powered brethren.

You be the judge.

Introduction

In introducing the basics of gliding, I will take this opportunity to give you an insight into some of the practical skills that you will need as you develop your interests and your careers.

Most of us start to teach ourselves when we leave school and it doesn't matter to me how long ago that was. Whatever age you have reached, if anyone offers help and guidance, grab the opportunity while you can. It is no crime to soak up all the knowledge you can on a subject and it is never too late to learn.

You will find no heavy formulae in this book, just the basic principles. In Britain, there is still a mix of imperial and metric units in use. Full-size glider flyers use the knot or nautical mile per hour for speed and rates of climb while talking about miles per hour on the road. Dimensions may be metric or imperial, so at this stage in your career, it will be helpful to be bilingual, so to speak.

The language of glider flyers and aeromodellers has its own vocabulary. In fact many sports and pastimes have invented their own words to describe things while some have been borrowed from elsewhere. I imagine that you know the difference between a football tackle and fishing tackle but where a term may be new to you, it has been *highlighted* and the text should provide sufficient information for you to understand what is meant by that word.

I hope that you will follow the book to the end and try some or all of the exercises. Take it all in, there are some questions for you to answer too. I have often quoted a training axiom that I picked up many years ago:

The greatest security is to be adaptable in a changing world.

It is pointless being a nuclear physicist if no one is building power stations and somewhere, there is a place for all of us. To help us find it, we need to be flexible and diverse in our background and I can think of no career which is not improved by a

Model or the real thing? The airbrakes may be out but the pilot of this Pilatus B4 would have had the retract down by now.

wider grasp of things mechanical and technical. With aviation, there is probably no other activity which covers such a wide variety of knowledge or such a challenge to the ability to learn.

There are already detailed books on such aspects as design, construction and flying techniques. The aim of this book is to try to show you some aspects of the challenges that gliding, whether real or modelling, can bring.

Enjoy it.

CHAPTER ONE

In the beginning

Birds have been soaring for millions of years — pterodactyls and the like long before that. All flying creatures evolved from those that moved in a denser media but nevertheless, where three dimension motion in water was very much akin to flying. The hows and whys are lost in the mysteries of evolution and perhaps without inspiration from the the birds we might never have thought flying was possible. No, surely we would.

First, you must realise that the average bird is a lazy little animal. They are conditioned to use whatever advantage moving air may give them in their continued quest for survival be it food, a mate or the sheer pleasure of being airborne. Since flying is about going up, then sinking air is of no interest to flying creatures and the search is rapidly moved elsewhere.

Bird evolution is a superb example of compromise at work and each species has now arrived at its optimum specification to fill the niche which nature has provided for it. Consider the influences which have shaped a wide variety of birds and jot down the main differences between say, a penguin, an albatross, a goose, domestic poultry, a sparrow, a kestrel and an eagle. Types and sizes of wings and feet determine how they move and where — and the type of beak determines what they feed on. If the bird has claws and a hooked beak, then you can be sure that it's not a duck...

Yes, the small birds such as skylarks using rising air but with a distinct shortage of span and wing area, show that gliding flight is not in their repertoire. First we will look at the means by which birds can prolong their flights without excess work and then compare some of the birds that take advantage of this ability. The two methods are:

Before mankind arrived, the first soarers were doing it their way. This is a model — and it flies.

Hill and cliff soaring. Where the wind is blowing onto a hill, it cannot blow through it and the air is deflected up and over. The rising air will carry a bird higher with minimum effort. This benefit is used by birds ranging from the skylark and the common crow to the Andean condor. This effect of air being deflected upwards can also be encountered miles out at sea where the albatross can soar indefinitely on air pushed upwards by a moving wave. Watch gulls soaring along sea walls or low sand dunes and it will be realised that the lift generated can be very strong

Thermal soaring. When air is warmed by the sun, it will expand and become lighter. Temperature differences between neighbouring patches of air will mean that the warmer, lighter air will break away first in a column or bubble and will start to rise. Birds are expert at reading the air to find upgoing lift.

Watch the pilots of hot air balloons who use this to the full by carrying their own hot air with them and heating it up as they go. A boat will float because the weight of the water that the hull displaces weighs as much as the boat. There is a fixed volume of air in the canopy of a hot air balloon and when the weight of the balloon and its load is less than the weight of the air that it displaces, the whole thing will become buoyant and float — through the air. That may be simplistic, but at least we have introduced the outside influences and we will look at these in more detail later in the book.

AND WHAT OF MAN?

From mythology, the story of Icarus and Daedalus and their ambitious escape from Minoan Crete could well have been based on early experiments, who knows? When the comparatively low technology of the early Rogallo winged hang {from the German 'hang' for cliff} gliders is considered, the techniques could well have been established some few thousand years ago. Such ingenious people as Leonardo Da Vinci had the ideas schemed out and the dream continued for centuries.

Our concept of flight had been perhaps distorted by perceptions of mankind flying like the birds and this is illustrated in almost every church by images of winged angels. In practice, to achieve flapping flight, the arm and chest muscles would probably need to be some seven or eight times larger to even get off the ground. This also presumes that lung efficiency and capacity would permit the expenditure of the energy necessary to achieve this.

Now, once the idea of flapping flight had been forgotten, the idea of prolonged gliding did begin to take a hold. It was not until many centuries later that gliding flight was achieved by Yorkshireman Percy Pilcher's coachman who had no control whatsoever over his fate. He had a good idea that he would be going down but little else. This was very much a one way trip down a gentle hill though it was realised that weight distribution was as important as the rudimentary steering which was based on the principle of the rudder as used on a boat.

Other experimenters realised the importance of control by twisting the wing and tail surfaces to obtain full manoeuvrability in three dimensions. After all, birds did it that way and it worked for them.

The means whereby flight has been achieved seem to have evolved to one main pattern and it looks like the concept of wings, fuselage and tail surfaces is established as the norm. It is an incredibly involved subject and this book won't teach you all about it, but it will give you a fair idea of the basics.

CHAPTER TWO

Time for a little theory?

The fundamental principle of gliding is that there is no engine. Yes, I know that you knew that. So what makes a glider fly? The answer is *gravity*. Throw anything up into the air and you can bet that it will slow down, stop and then start to fall, accelerating downwards as it goes. This is due the force of gravity which is written as *g*. The acceleration of a falling body in a vacuum would be 32 feet per second every second — more on that later. Since a glider cannot fly in a vacuum, that is academic anyway and the size and shape of a falling body determines how fast it will fall and where it will go.

For practical reasons, assume that gravity is the same everywhere on the surface of this planet. In reality, the higher you get, the less effective it becomes until, like the spaceman in orbit, there is no gravity and thus no apparent weight. For a glider to be practical, it needs to fly in a predetermined direction and have some in built *stability*. Too much stability and the glider is uncontrollable so basically, the aircraft needs some means of upsetting its natural path.

Look at the action of the *fin* and *rudder* first. The weather cock has one main characteristic and that is that there is a lot more side area on one side of the pivot point than the other. The bigger area is always the bit that trails downwind. An interesting thing for you to grasp at this stage is that of what engineers call *Moments*. No, not an instant of time but the force that a weight or an area has when moving against a pivot. You may know this as *leverage* and really it's the same thing, but get the terminology right and you will find it easier to talk the same language.

Bear with me while I explain from first principles. Mum takes the twins onto the see-saw at the park. Both sides are the

The top of that hill produces good soaring conditions. Those clouds could well indicate thermal lift.

same length and mum weighs twice as much as each twin. The see-saw will balance with a twin on either end, or both on one end and mum on the other. That set up does not mind how long the see-saw is but it does give the formula:

$$M_w \times L = 2 \times t_w \times L$$

M_w is mum's weight, t_w is the weight of a twin and L is half the length of the see saw. The moment is the force multiplied by the distance from the pivot. As a reminder, a force is written as a number followed by its units, i.e.., ten ounces, 144 square inches, one square foot. A *wing loading* would be a compound of that and be written as ten ounces per square foot. With a ten ounce per square foot loading, what would a model with a wing area of five square feet weigh? Now try it the other way.

For directional stability, the glider needs more area at the rear to keep the nose pointing where it is to go. It also needs a movable vertical surface to deflect it from its path. Right, that's the rudder and its force can be measured by its area times the distance from the balance point of the glider. Double the force by increasing the area or increasing the length of the fuselage — or some of each.

THE FUSELAGE.

This is provided for two reasons: to keep the wings and tailplane apart and for somewhere for the pilot to sit.

The glider also needs to balance front and rear and using the rules of moments, a heavy pilot and all the controls in a short cockpit at the front will be balanced by a

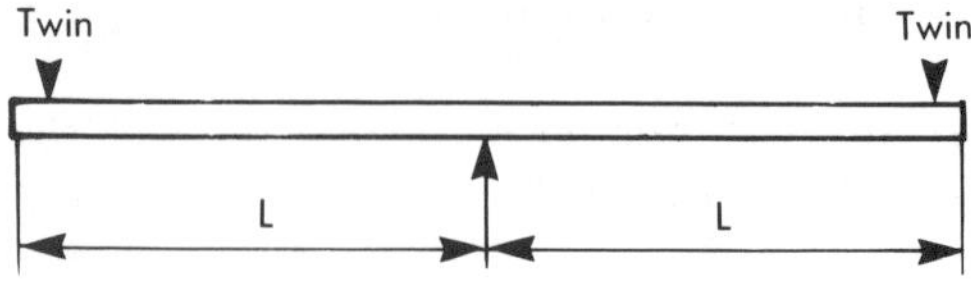

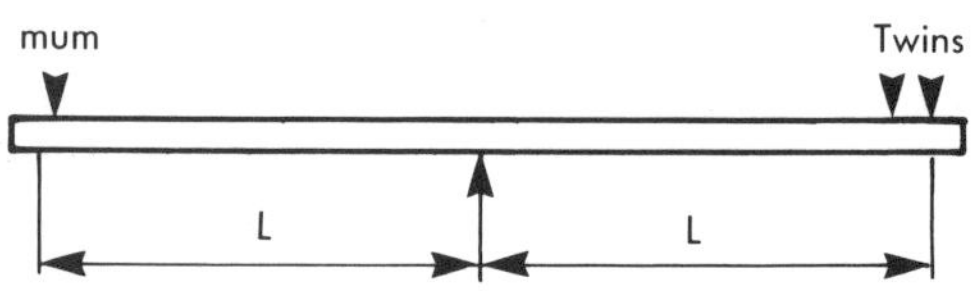

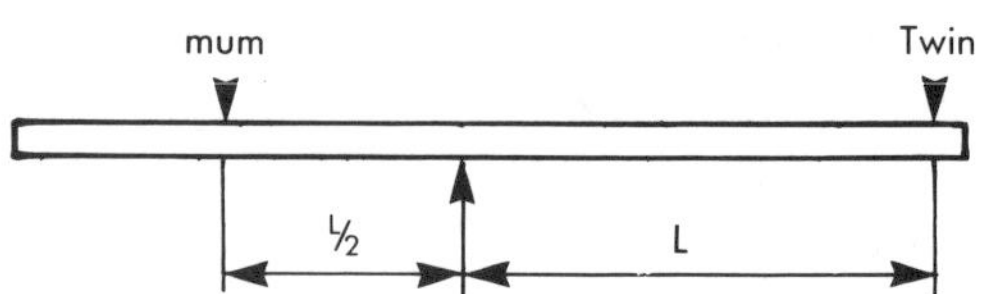

Figure 1. States of balance.
Force times distance = moment.

The usual shape shows elegantly tapered wing and fuselage with the control surfaces at a distance where they are most effective. This is a modern Mosquito. Note the large forward opening canopy and the retractable main wheel.

lighter tailplane right out at the back. The principle of moments also determines the size and shape of the fuselage. The further away from the structural centre, the less the moment and the less load that the fuselage needs to be able to stand. The reduction in cross sectional area is usually integrated into a rather pleasing and graceful shape.

Now where the glider should actually *balance* is a matter for a bit of aerodynamics and the rules change with different types of aerofoil sections and airframe arrangements. I will not cover pitching moments of aerofoils, just keep it in mind. You will have realised that in the same way that a rudder is needed to deflect the glider sideways, the tailplane will alter the angle at which the wing is presented to the airflow, *angle of attack* is how that is known and is not to be confused with *incidence* which is the difference in angles between the wings and tailplane. To correct any slight out of balance fore and aft, it is usual to wind the tail or elevator control surfaces in one direction or the other to achieve stable flight. Overall control still needs larger movements and again, using the principle of moments, the elevator can be made more powerful by making it bigger, or by making the fuselage longer.

Practical experience has provided all the answers so far and as layouts prove successful, their shapes become accepted. That brings up another axiom *'If it looks right, it is right'*. Don't use that expression in a modern aircraft factory, the designers use computers to tell them what every glider pilot knows by eye.

Now, it is possible to make a glider that is so stable that it will only fly in a straight line so some compromise must be made so that it can be steered in three dimensions. A glider that is very stable will require large movements of the control surfaces and will be very slow to react. Conversely, a glider which is almost totally unstable will require continual control inputs to prevent it from crashing.

WHAT ABOUT THE WINGS?

Without them you don't have a glider. The challenge is to fight gravity and descend to earth as slowly as possible – and in a controlled manner.

The function of the wing is to provide lift

Spread the load. Wing and tailplane taper clearly illustrated here.

to counter the downwards pull of gravity. The tailplane gives a stabilising effect which prevents the flight path being upset by gusts of wind while the elevator actually gives a positive effect on control by changing the attitude of the glider.

One thing that you will notice about a wing is that it has a particular shape. This is rounded at the front and tapering to a sharp edge at the rear, known as *leading edge* and *trailing edge* respectively. The thickest part of the wing is about one third the way back and it is at this point that the main load bearing member known as a *spar* is located.

You will also notice that most often, the wing tapers from the root to the tip and there are two main reasons for this. The main reason is perhaps structural and we again consider the matter of moments. A wing needs to be able to withstand the loads imposed upon it by launching and flying and we will consider just the mechanics of leverage. A load put upon a wing close to the root is measured as the force multiplied by the distance from the root. Since the load is proportional to the area, it will be seen that a constant chord width would produce a proportionally increasing load as it moves out towards the tip. The only thing to do is to reduce the wing area by reducing the chord which coincidentally also reduces the area and thus the load. This means that the spar can taper therefore there is less weight towards the tip which means that the spar has less work to do etc.

The second reason is a little less obvious and in the language of engineers, it is a problem known as *inertia*. This is the opposite to what it takes to get you out of bed in the mornings. If the glider is upset, it will continue to move in its deflected direction until corrected by a control input. If the extremes of the structure are heavy, they will want to keep on going in the wrong direction and the control movements will need to be so much greater with a consequent drag penalty. If the wing tips and the tail are light and the weight of the aircraft is all towards the centre, then it is not only easier to correct, it is more stable in the first place.

So, the fuselage will taper as will the wings, the rudder and the tailplane too and the shape starts to take on the familiar outline that we recognise.

CHAPTER THREE

Controls

There are two essentials in controlling a glider:

1. Have the appropriate control surfaces.
2. Have air flowing over them.

Park the glider on the ground and move the controls and you will realise that they are doing precisely nothing. With the glider in flight, there is sufficient air flowing past to give the controls something to work on. Air may be a gas but flying through it at 50 mph, it is pretty solid. Try standing up in a 50 mph wind.

The glider will have been designed to have an optimum flying speed and the *airspeed indicator* tells a full-size glider pilot what speed it is flying at.

On the wings, the control surfaces which roll the aircraft are known as *ailerons*. One moves upwards as the other goes downwards. The one that moves upwards pushes that wing downwards — helped by the other one pushing upwards of course. Often, the upgoing aileron will move twice as far as the downgoing one because any control surface movement produces drag and too much drag on the opposite side could in fact have the glider trying to turn the other way. This is known as adverse yaw which will be explained later.

The controls of a full-size glider have the control column moving right and left, forward and back or anywhere in that circle. The *elevator* controls the speed of

That's the main control stick between the pilot's knees. Rudder pedals by the feet — of course.

the glider, not whether it is climbing or diving. The glider does have an optimum speed and the elevator is used to control that. Move the stick forwards, the nose drops and the speed increases. Pull it back and the nose rises, the speed drops and the aircraft becomes uncontrollable. It is said to be *stalled*, then the nose drops with maybe a sideways twist as one wing stalls first and the glider falls until flying speed has been regained.

Making a turn essentially is a two control system combining ailerons and elevator. Move the stick to the right, the right aileron goes up pushing that wing down and rolling it about the central axis. It would continue in a straight line for a while before falling sideways but while it is banked over, the elevator will now act as a rudder. Pull back on the stick while the glider is banked over and the result will be a banked turn. Centralise the control stick and you return to level flight.

So what's the rudder for? Glad you asked. The back end of the fuselage will always lag behind the glider when making a turn and the glider will be trying to turn with the fuselage sideways on to the line of flight. The rudder pedals are pushed in the direction of the turn at the same time as the ailerons are moved and the fuselage kicks smartly out to smoothly follow the glider's path.

Just kicking the rudder over as the glider is flying straight and level causes the aeroplane to fly somewhat sideways. This is not good and the usual trick is to fasten a piece of wool on the outside of the canopy to tell the pilot to do something about it. Opposite rudder straightens it up.

I must mention here that in addition to the controls already described, the glider usually has some built in stability known as *dihedral*. This is the shallow vee that the wings show when viewed from the front. This will ensure that the centre of lift is well above the centre of gravity of the glider giving a self stabilising effect. Just a bit like a pendulum maybe but it also improves turn response. The effect of the rudder is to

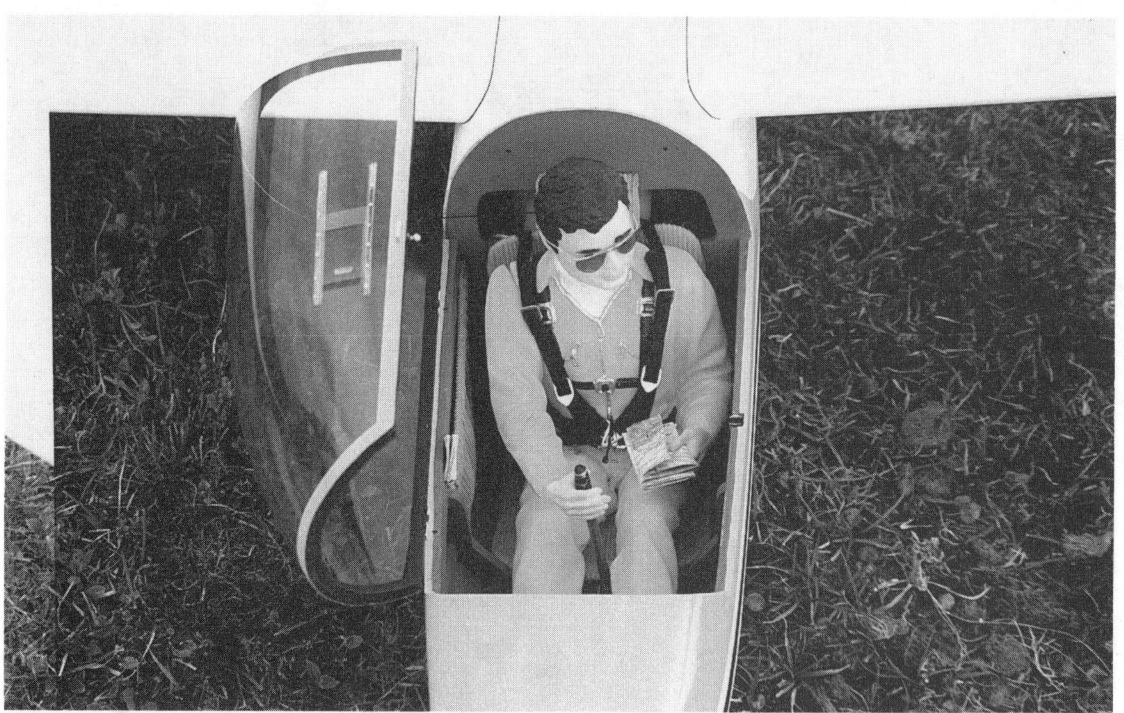

This model cockpit even has its own column. Superb detail.

turn the aeroplane sideways (yaw, remember?) and this moves one wing forward and the other backwards to the direction of flight. The wing pointing forwards will generate more lift producing a bank and assisting the turn.

In fact with sufficient dihedral, ailerons would not be essential in steering a glider at all. Fine if you were flying in smooth air but ailerons do give total control in all three axes, essential in a full-size glider and in turbulent conditions. Many model aircraft however, fly quite satisfactorily using rudder and elevator alone. In fact the elevator is not essential except to give nicety of pitch control and to increase speed when penetrating back upwind.

For full-size sailplanes incidentally, it is worth having a look at the Microsoft Flight Simulator programme available for IBM computers. In among a selection of powered aircraft, you will find programmes for thermal soaring and also ridge soaring which have a fairly good 'feel' to them. Nothing like doing it for real though.

Those are the controls used by full size glider pilots who can feel the motion of the glider and take instant action — just like birds can. These are also the controls used by model aircraft flyers so let's check that you have grasped that so far. Here is a simple design which will allow you to examine the effects of the controls and factors which influence stability. The drawing is to a reduced scale and it is expected that you will draw it, cut out and glue it accurately. A sheet of 1.5mm balsa will make a few. Take the trouble to sand it properly and make a good job of it. Remember, measure twice and cut once.

Trimming is simple. Just balance the model where shown with a paper clip, modelling clay or whatever until the glider flies in an even straight line. Unless you are trying this indoors and hit some furniture, it is unlikely that the test model will be broken.

Try these simple control experiments:

1. Bend the rudder one way. Just enough and the glider will circle that way, too much and it will spiral down as the model banks and the rudder becomes down elevator. This is opposite to the elevator in the earlier example isn't it?

Can't miss that airfield but land too far away from the retrieving crew and you would not be very popular.

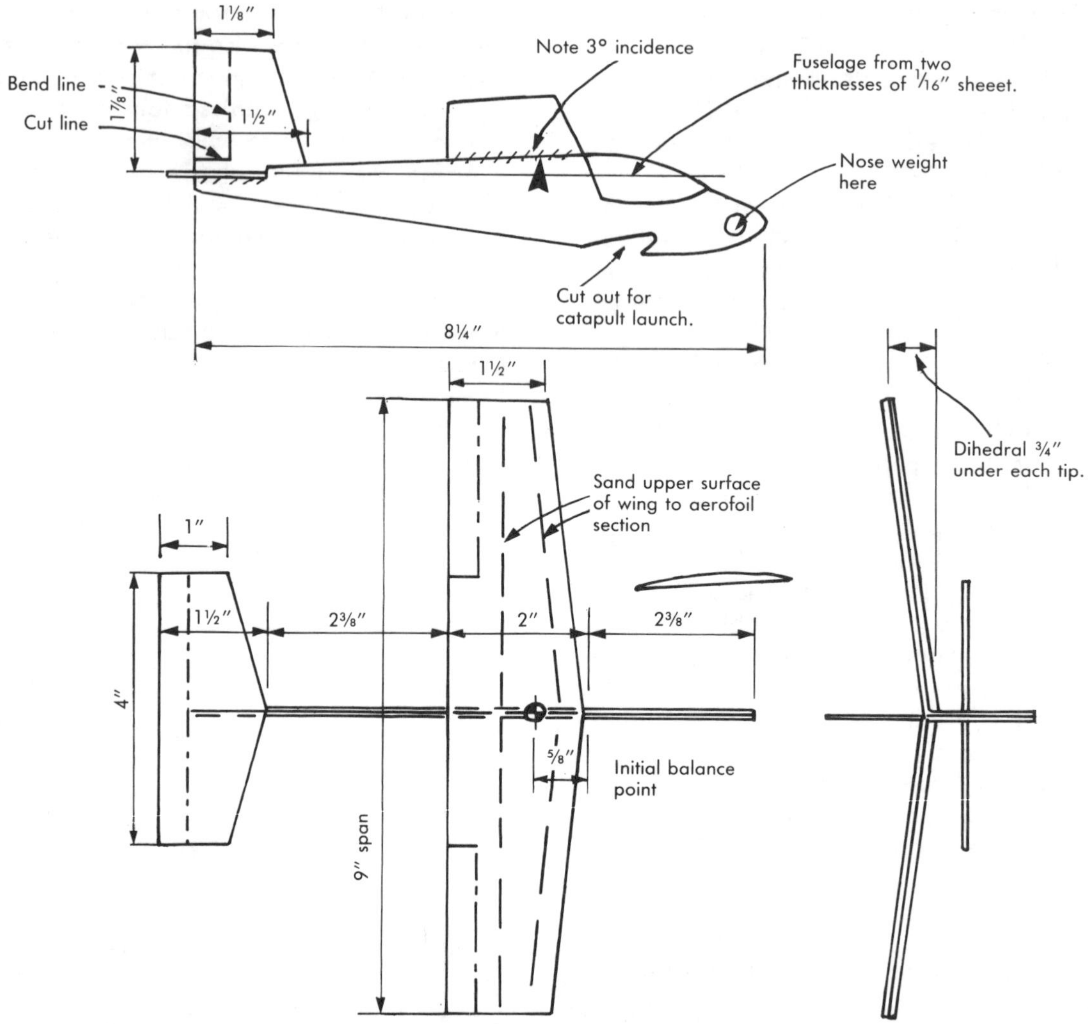

Figure 2. 'Controls' test model from ¹⁄₁₆″ sheet balsa — Dimensions are nominal only.

This is the control exercise model. No need to overdo the stretch.

2. Straighten the rudder and bend the elevator down. Watch it dive.
3. Bend the elevator up. With enough speed, the glider will loop and as the speed falls off, it will lose flying speed, stall and drop to the ground.
4. Straighten up and trim for a nice flat glide again. Now raise the right aileron and depress the left one by half that amount. Throw the glider fast and watch it roll.
5. As before but depress the left aileron by twice the amount of the right hand one. Would you expect it to roll faster? No, the left hand one generates more drag and the model will no doubt fall to the left.
6. Trim for a flat glide again, then remove the weight from the nose and launch the model. What happened?
7. What happens if you add more weight to the front of the model without altering the control surface settings?

CHAPTER FOUR

A bit of aerodynamics

For a wing to generate lift, there must be an airflow over it and the perhaps over-simplified reason is that with an aerofoil section as shown in Fig. 3, the airflow is deflected both over and under the wing though you will see that the air moving over the top has farther to go than the air following the straighter path along the underside. Since this air is 'stretched', it is less dense and therefore the air underneath will want to move up to balance it. It can't because there is a wing in the way, so it pushes up the wing instead. Over simple? Wait for it.

Aerofoil sections come in many forms and again, every one of them is a compromise. A slow flying training glider may be required simply to find its way to earth and demonstrate the means of control to its pilot. A performance glider will be required to move swiftly between thermals and yet be able to slow down in order to circle tightly when lift has been found. To do this, special aerofoil sections have been developed in which about one fifth of the rear of the wing can be deflected both upwards and downwards to change the characteristics of that section. This part of the wing is known as a *flap*, it may run the whole length of the wing and incorporate the ailerons as well.

As I said earlier, for a wing or control surface to work, there must be forward motion or airspeed. If there is no *airspeed*, then two things will happen:

(a) the control surfaces will become useless and
(b) the glider will fall out of the sky.

The correct amount of forward speed is determined by the weight of the glider and the type of wing section used.

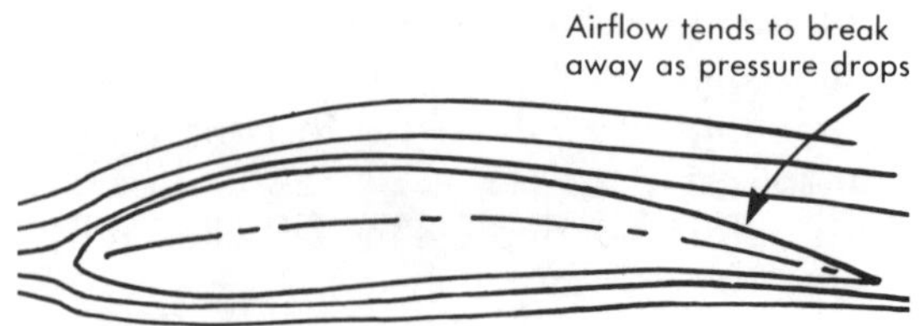

Figure 3. Typical airflow over section.

Air is perceived as slipping over the surface of the wing skin in layers, actually an infinite number of layers which calculus covers quite well. A smooth airflow is required over the skin and it is desirable to extend this *laminar flow* right to the trailing edge.

When the airflow is smooth, the glider can be a very efficient flying machine. Slow it down too much and the smooth airflow over the wing breaks down causing lots of drag hauling the glider to a rapid stop. This is very embarrassing if you are at 1000 feet but more so if you are much less than 500 feet since you will not have enough height to regain flying speed. The landing will be painful or expensive or both. Worse, you might never feel the pain or have to pay for the repairs.

Flying too slow is not the only problem that a glider pilot may face. Imagine diving down from a great height and accelerating under the pull of gravity, *g*, remember? The aeroplane can accelerate to the speed where the structure cannot stand the loads that are being imposed on it, the wings and control surfaces could start to flutter and the glider will begin to break up. There are few things more embarrassing than being up high without a glider or a parachute. Glider manufacturers thus decide what speeds are safe and you must follow their

The airbrakes can be seen open on this shot. They may look small but they are very effective.

rules. The minimum speed is the *Stalling* speed, the maximum safe speed is known as *VNE* or *velocity never exceed*. You see, you have to do it right.

Many gliders are very efficient with a fast flat glide and slowing down for a landing could be very difficult. Precise landings are essential of course and for this purpose, the glider is equipped with *airbrakes*. These take different forms but all have one thing in common; they destroy the smooth airflow over the wing. Letter box slots, flat plates that pivot upwards, trailing edge flaps that hang down — you imagine it, it's been tried.

CHAPTER FIVE

A bit more technical

The forces that act on a glider in flight are many and the usual form is to illustrate them as the downward pull due to gravity, upward thrust due to lift from the wings and a rearward component due to the *drag* of the air.

You will get an idea of the effect of drag by moving an oar in water edgeways on — it slips through easily. Flatways on and the weight of water that it tries to displace is sufficient to move the boat. With an aircraft, drag is even more complex because there is friction between the skin and the air, this is why the space shuttle needs heat resistant tiles as friction heats up the skin. All the changes in shape and the air that is displaced to allow the passage of the aircraft has to be paid for in energy, that is *parasitic drag*. The efficiency loss in making the wing work is called *profile drag*.

It is mainly drag that pulls a glider down and the force that it exerts can be measured at different speeds, pressures and humidities. A glider being released from a certain height has only so much potential energy and it is expensive to waste this displacing air. Drag can be measured at various flying speeds and with only so much potential energy available, it should be possible to work out the optimum flying speed for the glider.

An assessment of the efficiency of a glider is in its claimed *glide angle*, that is how far it can travel for the loss of a unit of height. A good training glider will be about 30 to 1, while a super slick ship will be 50 or more. The minimum sink rate, in other words, how long it will stay up from a certain height is not necessarily at this glide angle or flying speed but that one will have to keep.

Aerofoil sections are designed for certain applications and Fig. 4 shows some typical shapes that they take. The main identifier of an aerofoil section is the *camber*. A line drawn from the front of the radius of the leading edge to the rear point of the trailing edge is the camber line and this actually follows the thickness of the aerofoil as it changes. The camber line is in fact halfway between the upper and lower surfaces, and in a *symmetrical* section will be a straight line from front to back. Now bend this line and you will see that it eventually becomes flatter underneath, even more and the undersurface becomes concave. This section would then be referred to loosely as *undercambered*. The latter would have a high *coefficient of lift* (C_l) but the drag would be unnecessarily high at the range of speeds that we consider as suitable for our activities. Another term that you will eventually come to know with aerofoil sections is the *neutral point* which is tied in with *pitching moments* at differing

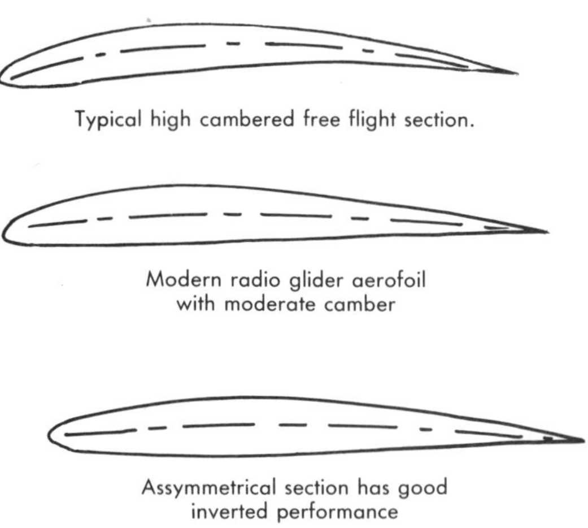

Figure 4. Typical aerofoil shapes. Camber line is mid way between upper and lower skins.

speeds — have fun with that later when you start to investigate centre of gravity locations and other factors influencing stability.

Aerofoil sections to your own sizes can be drawn out from *co-ordinates* provided in table form. These figures are for points in the x, y axes system and are written as a percentage of the desired wing *chord* width. Thus, a point is located by x along and y up from the datum line which is drawn first. Where y is given as a minus number, that point is below the line. Fig. 5a lists *ordinates* for a popular wing section. As an exercise, draw this out to use as a basis for the glider projects later. This aerofoil is one originated by Doctor Eppler and has proved to be very successful in general soaring models. It is designated E193 and you will see that there is a slight concavity on the underside. For practical purposes, you may draw a line straight across as this will then permit the wing to be built flat on a board.

Plotting out the points on squared paper and using a French curve to join up the points is a useful way to start. When you have mastered that, you may be interested to know that there are computer programmes available from Nexus that will draw out aerofoil sections, calculate any changes that you want such as percentage thickness, blend with other sections and predict performances.

Surprisingly, unlike the example of the oar, a sharp leading edge is no advantage since that only works in one plane. An aircraft wing needs to be able to provide lift at minimum drag and over a wide range of flying speeds. A rounded leading edge enables a wider range of angles of attack to be used without the air breaking away uncontrollably from the front.

The speed and lift generated does depend upon the angle at which it is presented to the airflow and this is controlled by the tailplane. Wind tunnel tests show exactly what is going to happen as this angle increases until it reaches the stage when, just like the oar, it can no

longer move forward. Long before that happened, the wing would cease to provide lift and the glider would stall and fall out of the sky. The airflow over a wing is subject to turbulence and ideally, should flow sweetly and the perfect condition would be where the airflow would separate at the leading edge and rejoin at the trailing edge with no turbulence at all. Usually, the airflow will begin to separate from the wing between half and two thirds the way back and research continues in this direction.

When the airflow does break away lift is destroyed and the glider will drop. However, the stall may not occur over all the wing at once. Most often, particularly with a high aspect ratio glider where the outer wing tip is flying much faster than the inner, the airflow over the slower tip might break away earlier and that wing will drop first. Down elevator, opposite rudder, lots of height and a bit of luck come in useful here. The most important thing is never to fly too slowly.

The other drag problem is that as the wing is creating lift, there is a sideways motion towards the tip where air spills over and creates a vortex. This is the twisting column of air that you can see on an approaching passenger jet or as vapour trails across the sky. Little winglets may be used to help control this effect and sailplane designers also counter this problem by building the wing so that it twists upwards towards the wing tip. This is known as *washout* and it will bring the stalling point further inboard. Too slow and it will still stall, but hopefully across the whole of the span and a straight ahead recovery will be possible.

A change of wing section towards the tip may provide some additional safety though the risk may still be there. This is one of the penalties of a long thin wing which has a higher efficiency. The *wing span* divided by the mean or average wing *chord* (width) is known as the *aspect ratio*, a training glider may be around 10 to 1 while a high performance glass sailplane may be 30 or more. A glass composite wing with a high aspect ratio can be a frightening thing to see at first since it will flex such that it seems it would fail.

A final point about drag is in the application of airbrakes. It is pointless locking the wheel if it is not touching the ground. Spoiling the airflow hauls the glider earthwards quite quickly and a change of trim may be needed to keep up the flying speed as the glide angle steepens and the rate of descent increases. Too slow an approach can be dangerous as even a large glider can face problems with turbulence on final approach and it comforting to know that your arch enemy, drag, can in fact be your best friend when you are trying to get down safely.

From the cockpit

The pilot has instruments to tell him what *airspeed* he is flying at and in which direction. It is airspeed that is important and not *groundspeed*. If a glider is flying at 50 knots into a 20 knot wind, the groundspeed would appear to be 30 knots. Flying downwind, the groundspeed would be more like 70 knots.

You see why aircraft should always land into the wind. It's easier on the brakes and you can use a shorter runway. Easy, but some people who should know better…

The *compass* is the device used to tell the pilot which direction he is heading in and helps him find the airfield. He also has a device known as a *variometer* which measures minute changes in air pressure and tells the pilot whether the glider is climbing or sinking. If you close your eyes and try to balance on one leg, you might guess what the other instruments are for. When flying an aeroplane in cloud with no ground reference point to be seen, it is quite possible to find yourself flying upside down. The *turn and slip indicators* are there to tell you exactly what is going on and these are instruments that you ignore at your peril.

The instruments are a part of the pre-flight check procedure and as the pilot readies, the following is going through his mind; CB − SIF − CB. This is the mnemonic for:

Canopy, closed and secure.
Ballast, to make up for solo pilot in a twin seater or a lightweight.

The flying instructor takes a laid back attitude to the would be pilot's final checks.

A modern instrument panel. Cable release on left, rate of climb or sink at top alongside airspeed indicator. Altimeter and turn and slip indicators useful when you can't see the ground.

Straps, harness buckled up properly, like a bandage, firm but not too tight.

Instruments, in apparent good condition.

Flaps, where fitted should be free to operate.

Controls, rudder pedals and stick move freely to the limits of their travels with no restrictions, tightness or slop in their movements. The trim lever is set to neutral.

Brakes, these should open and close smoothly.

The final check is done by the launch crew who hang on the cable which may be pulled by a ground winch or by aircraft. Aerotow is effective in getting the glider to the required height and can even be beneficial in taking the glider under the cumulus clouds which may signal the presence of thermals, but it can add to the cost of your flying.

A signal to the winch man or tow tug pilot has the call of "Up slack", a nod of approval and the shout is "All out" and the glider rapidly accelerates to take off speed. A winch launch needs up elevator to *rotate* and get the nose up. Rudder control is used to keep the nose straight up the line.

The winch man decides when to let off the power and two tugs on the release knob makes sure that the glider is free as the line drops away.

An aerotow needs the glider pilot to follow slightly above the tug and on release, the drill is to break away in different direcions,.

Now, you are by yourself.

CHAPTER SEVEN

What about model gliders?

There is a lot to learn and an apprenticeship served with model aircraft is not a bad idea. The principles are about the same and the expense and fun factor are every bit as high. Should you decide to go on to full-size aviation, then the experience will be of great benefit. Otherwise, the hobby and indeed sport will be of enormous pleasure and will generate its own circle of friends for you.

In the days before reliable radio control equipment, it seemed that there were more people flying free-flight models. Free flight however is again becoming more popular and it is an excellent way of learning many of the skills necessary to get a foothold in the sport. Remember the trimming techniques from Chapter 3? The free-flight model is set to fly in a stable condition so that it will fly by itself without any other control. The models are usually set to circle but need a good sized space in which to fly. Any free-flight model will drift downwind so it is necessary to have a space clear of houses and trees and to be able to run after it. Even a flat calm day may have some drift so be sure which way it will be heading.

Later, you will find details of a simple free-flight glider that will not take too much of your time or resources and will introduce you to some of the skills which you will need as you progress. There are suitable kits readily available which are comparatively inexpensive though a class project could cut the overall cost. The West Wings Merlin at 35'' span is a useful alternative while the Nexus plans service has dozens to choose from. A few are listed in the appendix.

These models do not use ailerons, we will come to that later with the second stage of radio control. Can't wait? You'd better.

Balsa wood is still the easiest material to use since it cuts, glues and sands well. It is light enough and has been the most popular material for model aircraft since it was introduced in the 1920s. Being porous, it readily accepts most glues and the basic technique for construction is simply to cut adjacent faces as accurately as possible, apply just enough glue to wet both and push them together. Depending on what sort of glue you use, you may secure the two pieces together with a straight pin until the joint is set. Water based PVA or aliphatic glue is ideal and is cheaper than the solvent based balsa cements which we used as kids.

The only part of building this model that you might find boring is having to make a template and cutting out a set of wing ribs. It is however, part of the job and it is easier to do it right in the first place than spoil it and have to start again. Patience is a virtue.

Your local model shop will have all the materials that you may need including tissue and dope or covering film. You may also get some help and advice but the best way forward is to make contact with a local club whose members will generally be delighted to help. Craft and Design Technology students may be following this book as part of a project and in which case, will help each other. Your local club will still be a good place to make contact though. A stamped, self addressed envelope to one of the addresses listed in the appendix will get you all the help you can cope with.

This is the Nomadix. Get help if you need it.

The previous test model that you made could have been drawn straight onto the sheet balsa. With the second design which you will find on Fig. 5, try drawing it out as a full size plan on a piece of paper. Any plain paper will do, even A4 sheets taped together and if you have access to a drawing board and set square, so much the better.

Working from a plan, particularly for wings and tailplanes is of enormous help as you will have an instant check that everything is being built properly. Where the glue joints are going to be, rub the paper with the end of a candle to stop things sticking to the plan and use straight pins to hold the bits in place. Do give the glue plenty of time to harden before you try to move it too or you will find yourself having to pin it down again.

Wing construction is a good place to start and it is important to remember that it is the covering material that gives the final shape and rigidity. Covering does not hide constructional faults and there is only one way to do it and that is the right way. Take the trouble to make a sound job of construction, a poor joint may not show under the covering but when it fails, everything will be open to inspection. My models may not always be pretty but they do not fall apart in the air...

Figure 5 (right). Nomadix — A simple free-flight glider for you to draw full size.

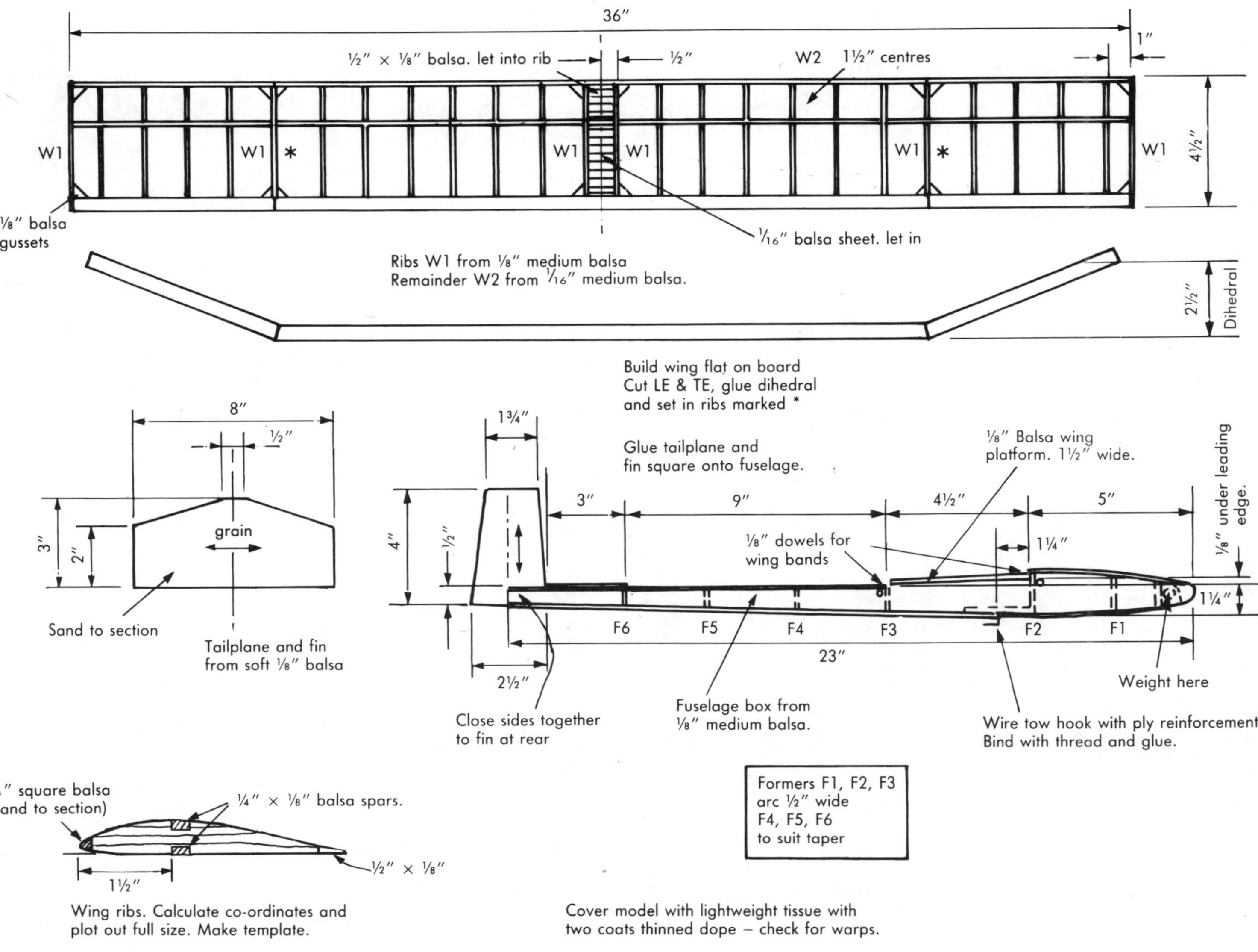
36"
1"
½" × ⅛" balsa. let into rib
½"
W2 1½" centres
4½"
W1
W1
*
W1
W1
W1
*
W1
⅛" balsa gussets
1/16" balsa sheet. let in
Ribs W1 from ⅛" medium balsa
Remainder W2 from 1/16" medium balsa.
2½"
Dihedral
Build wing flat on board
Cut LE & TE, glue dihedral
and set in ribs marked *
8"
½"
grain
3"
2"
Sand to section
Tailplane and fin
from soft ⅛" balsa
1¾"
4"
½"
2½"
Close sides together
to fin at rear
Glue tailplane and
fin square onto fuselage.
3"
9"
4½"
5"
⅛" Balsa wing platform. 1½" wide.
⅛" dowels for wing bands
1¼"
1¼"
⅛" under leading edge.
F6
F5
F4
F3
F2
F1
23"
Fuselage box from ⅛" medium balsa.
Weight here
Wire tow hook with ply reinforcement.
Bind with thread and glue.
Formers F1, F2, F3
arc ½" wide
F4, F5, F6
to suit taper
¼" square balsa (sand to section)
¼" × ⅛" balsa spars.
1½"
½" × ⅛"
Wing ribs. Calculate co-ordinates and
plot out full size. Make template.
Cover model with lightweight tissue with
two coats thinned dope – check for warps.

Cord Station	Upper Surface	Chord Station	Lower Surface
XU	YU	XL	YL
.000	.000	.000	.000
.026	.190	.129	−.375
.465	.915	.819	−.838
1.344	1.740	2.044	−1.252
2.652	2.608	3.791	1.588
4.383	3.487	6.049	−1.841
6.525	4.352	8.801	−2.010
9.061	5.181	12.026	−2.098
11.967	5.957	15.697	+2.112
15.218	6.663	19.778	−2.061
18.780	7.284	24.227	−1.955
22.620	7.805	28.998	−1.807
26.696	8.213	34.035	−1.628
30.967	8.487	39.280	−1.430
35.402	8.603	44.672	−1.244
39.979	8.551	50.145	−1.019
44.673	8.332	55.630	−.824
49.458	7.954	61.059	−.645
54.306	7.436	66.384	−.486
59.185	6.808	71.479	−.350
64.052	6.112	76.339	−.239
68.839	5.381	80.882	−.153
73.484	4.642	85.050	−.091
77.923	3.914	88.788	−.049
82.096	3.214	92.048	−.018
85.945	2.558	94.794	.010
89.414	1.957	97.003	.032
92.452	1.415	98.640	.034
95.023	.932	99.655	.014
97.108	.522	100.00	.000
98.674	.220		
99.661	.051		
100.00	.000		

Figure 5a. Ordinates for Eppler 193.

CHAPTER EIGHT

Construction exercises

When building any structure, it is useful to know why we do things a certain way and a few simple examples will serve to illustrate some theories of structures.

The shape of the *wing ribs* is what gives the aerofoil shape and it is important to check that they do not have any rough projections sticking up to spoil the smooth line of the covering. It is very easy to get this right by keeping the knife vertical and following the line accurately. Make a sandwich of the wing ribs, lightly sand to follow the template and they should be accurate enough for anyone. While the ribs are in a sandwich, make the cut outs for the spars to the exact width and depth. Do it accurately and the wing will be a pleasure to build.

The *spars* have an important function in that they provide some strength against bending. An interesting test is to take a piece of the spar material and bend it. Take two pieces and glue them together and you will find that sideways, they are just as flexible. Against two though, they are becoming quite stiff. Try again with two pieces and glue short lengths in between as spacers making the two strips even further apart and they become even stiffer.

The wing ribs take the part of the spacers and the wing becomes quite strong. In fact the leading and trailing edges do not contribute a great deal to the strength of the wing but it does need to support the covering and prevent damage in handling. Before we leave that test piece on spars, here is an exercise for you to try: Make a section of spar as shown in Fig. 6 with spacers glued in between. Let it dry properly and hold the ends firmly between fingers and thumbs. Push steadily with your thumbs and something will break. It may

Spar and wing rib construction can be seen clearly in the shot of an early Minimoa. Don't start on one of these.

flex a little but eventually, it will break. It will always follow the same form, one spar will fail in *compression* and will have three fractures, one in and two out. The other

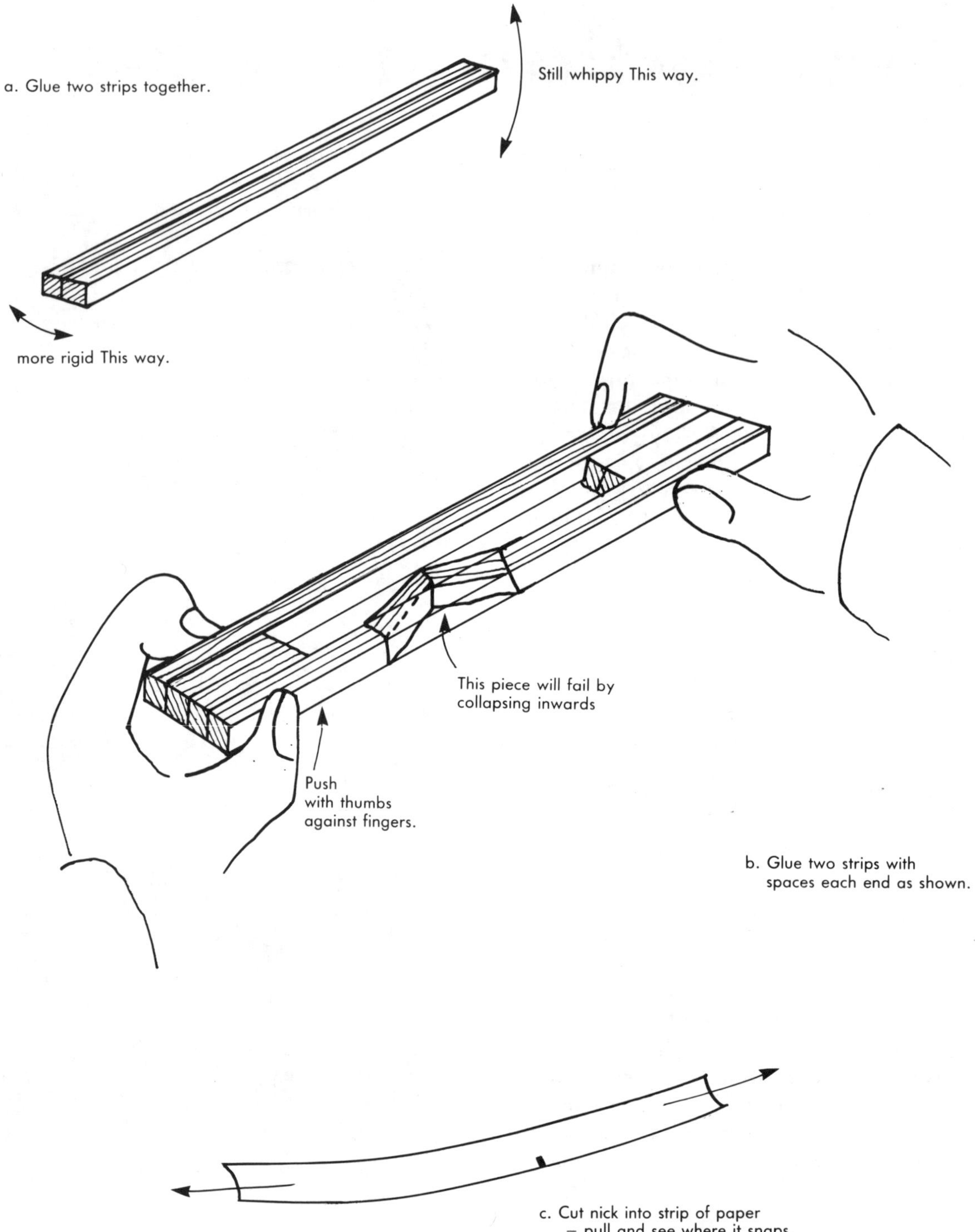

Figure 6. Make these test pieces to prove the point.

side will bend or possibly break against one of the cross pieces. This is because all the loads are concentrated at the place where strengthening is built in and any sudden change of cross section is known as a *stress raiser*.

To illustrate this, cut a strip of paper 1'' wide using scissors or a sharp knife. Pull evenly until it snaps. Where did it part? Cut another piece and make a nick say, 1/4'' wide somewhere in the middle and pull it again. It will snap of course. Guess where? Fuselages are subject to the same type of failures and you will find many examples in nature. Bend a drinking straw and you will find that one side collapses inwards. Convinced? When a wing is flexed upwards,

the lower spar and bottom skin are always in tension and this also applies to any other form of construction.

Tools you will need to start are a good sharp craft knife, a Stanley knife or scalpel is a good buy. A junior hack saw is handy for the jobs that would break your scalpel blades. A steel rule doubles for measuring and also as a straight edge to cut along. A small hand drill is useful along with screwdrivers and a light soldering iron. Most things you should have access to but materials, glue, pins and covering are all that you will need besides. All the instructions that you will need are on the following pages, get cracking.

CHAPTER NINE

Flying the free-flight glider

Whichever free-flight glider you decide upon on, the trimming and flying techniques are going to be the same.

Add lead shot or modelling clay to get the right balance and try a hand launch from shoulder height into wind. If it is set up right, it should glide straight and true.

Gliders do not have to look all the same. Flying wings give room for experimentation.

Rudder trim is as you would imagine but there is no elevator so a little piece of balsa or cardboard under the tailplane will be the way to change the trim. You have no ailerons to worry about, this model is going to fly itself and the trimming methods detailed earlier are what you will need to get the model to take care of itself.

Launching is a two handed job. You will be upwind on the end of a length of heavy thread while a friend holds the model. At a signal, run steadily forward and pull the model out of your helper's hands. Don't let him run after you as you need some tension to start the model climbing. You have built this glider so you have a fair idea of how strong it is. Should the tension on the line feel too much, slow down, if it is slack, change up a gear. If it veers off to one side, run that way but it should climb quite straight. When it gets to the top of the line, slackening off should allow the ring to release from the hook and the model will be free to glide by itself. Adjustments to the rudder will affect the glide circle but do it a little at a time until it is circling steadily and not so tight that it is spiralling in.

SOMETHING ELSE

Before you grow out of this glider try to launch it off a slope. Add a bit of balsa sheet to the fin as shown in Fig. 7 and when there is a light breeze blowing squarely on to a small hill or embankment, launch the glider into wind. If it blows back over your head, add some lead as close to the balance point as possible and try again. The glider should head out but ideally, if

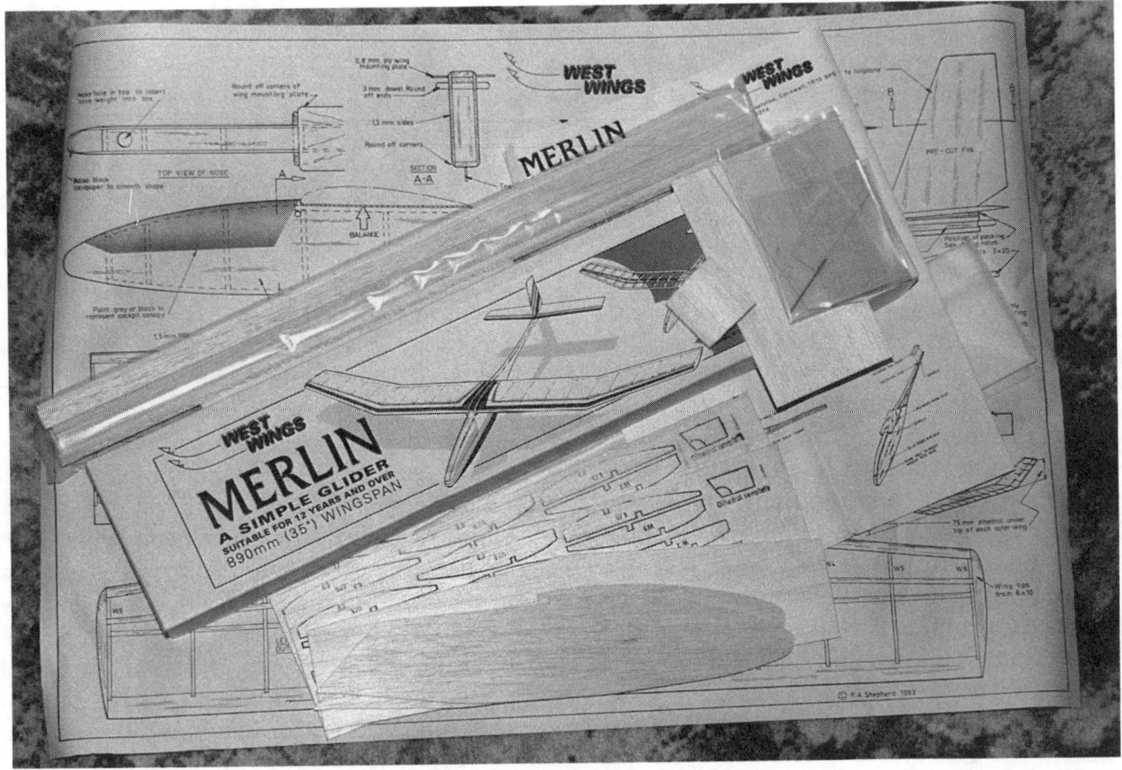

This is a typical beginner's kit. All the parts are there, just add skill.

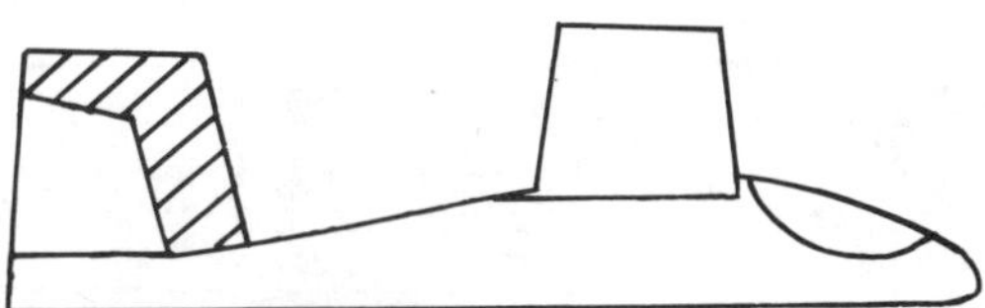

Figure 7. Added fin area moves centre of lateral area back — helps weathercock effect.

you have got the weight right to suit the wind speed, it should hover nicely into wind and achieve quite a long flight. Too much weight and it will end up down the bottom of the hill. Enjoy the walk.

What you have learned here is that a heavy glider will fly faster than a light one and sometimes, extra weight is used to help it fly in a strong wind. Not so important with a free-flight model since they all go downwind at the same rate regardless of what they weigh. Important though with a radio controlled glider or a full size which may need to penetrate forwards into wind or to fly long distances as fast as possible.

When you have achieved a prolonged flight, you can say that you have experienced the joys of slope soaring.

It's even more fun when you have control.

CHAPTER TEN

Radio control

The use of radio control equipment is the next development in your flying career.

Most people have at least some experience of remote control even if it is only the hand set for the tv. The profusion of radio control cars and boats has introduced many to the principles if not at first hand and the system is here to stay.

With a radio controlled car, there is a throttle or speed controller which may give some finesse but essentially, it gives also forward and reverse. Not many gliders fly backwards, in fact I can't think of any, but they do have the need to alter the forward speed and this we do with the elevator trim. The rudder is of course equivalent to the steering wheel.

You may know that when the car is moving away from you, the steering works as right for right but when the car, boat or plane is coming towards you, the control is reversed. Of course you knew that but in case you didn't, an electric car will help you get some practice in at zero risk. The throttle, forward and reverse or elevator for the glider does not change — unless the model is flying inverted of course. Aerobatics we will come to later.

The *transmitter* has control sticks which equate to the joystick on the full-size glider. There are also *secondary trims* which can be used to set the hands-off trim — just the same as full size too. The aerial is fully extended in use and for model gliders, the average radio transmitter has sufficient power to give solid control as far as you can see it. Even farther upwards, so you can pretty well reckon that if you can see it, you can fly it.

The *radio frequency* is varied by altering a small *crystal* in the transmitter and the *receiver*. These simply plug in with two pins

Typical standard, computerised and two channel transmitters. Note control sticks on the front of each case.

and it is a simple matter to check other frequencies on site and change if necessary. A *pennant* must be carried on the transmitter to indicate the frequency in use and a *peg system* is a help in avoiding any clashes. If another set with the same frequency as the one you are flying on is switched on, the model in the air will simply lock up so some discipline is essential.

While the frequency describes the carrier wave, the number of controls that a transmitter can handle is referred to as *channels*. The transmitter may be able to control say six operations, but if the glider is only using rudder and elevator, the glider is referred to as a two channel model.

The control surfaces on the model may be moved by sticks on the transmitter, but other controls such as airbrakes or flaps may use switches or knobs driving the servo/s to a pre-set position. Whatever your transmitter is supplied with has probably evolved in practice and while you might be able to improve something, it is most unlikely. The *receiver* looks like a small box with a length of wire trailing out behind. This is the *aerial* and should always be stretched out and not coiled up in the fuselage. Connections are provided for the *servos* which are geared electric motors which follow the signals sent out by your transmitter. *Proportional control* means that if you move a stick a little one way, the output arm on the servo will follow it. A centralising spring on the stick means that all will return to neutral when the stick is released.

The *frequency* used for model cars and boats is *27 megaherz* and there is no legal restriction on your use of that frequency. There is however a risk that any other user that you cannot see may not be aware that you are there and shoot your glider down. *35 megaherz* is the frequency allocated to the flying of radio controlled models and there is probably less chance of being shot down on this frequency when it is used carefully.

Second-hand equipment can be bought at a reasonable price with the advantage that in the unlikely event that you do not take to the sport, then it could probably be sold for what you paid for it...

The batteries which you might use are generally rechargeable.

Nickel cadmium is the general name and your fellow radio control enthusiasts refer to these as *nicads*. They will usually stand a lot of abuse but you must regularly check the condition of each cell and the wiring harness. There are many different types of chargers from constant current to those that will sense a battery's condition and treat it accordingly. Some will discharge the battery and then recharge it from scratch. We have the technology...

The transmitter could control a number of servos so rudder, elevator, ailerons, even airbrakes, flaps and a retractable landing wheel are possible. It is possible to mix functions electronically and you will learn eventually that there is so much more to be done than simple control.

Conventions for setting up radio control of gliders are divided two ways, which you use is a matter of preference and may be influenced by which way you are taught. It is usual to have the primary control (rudder or ailerons) on the right hand stick with the movement being *right for right* as with a full-size glider. The elevator may also be on that same stick pulling back towards you for up elevator and forward for down. The elevator could well be on the other stick which is where you will place the rudder if ailerons are used, as they then become the primary control. Fig. 8 shows how.

Should you be using a two channel set as with your electric car, the chances are that you will have rudder or ailerons on the right stick and elevator on the left. Actually, you won't have a lot of choice. What you need to be able to do is to make the correct control inputs without having to think about it. Practice and your reactions will become automatic.

As you develop, it will be an advantage to be able to use either method in flying

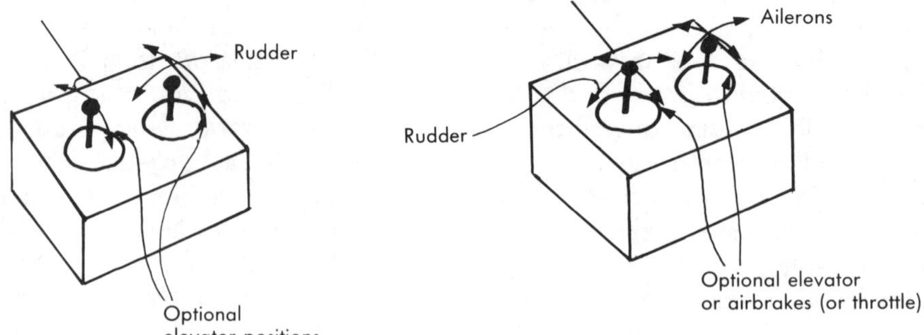

Figure 8. A couple of variations on transmitter set up.

other models and helping others to learn. Oh yes, learning. There is a system by which the learner's transmitter can be coupled to that of the teacher. One battery only is in use and a micro switch means that if the beginner gets into trouble, the teacher lets go of the switch and regains control. The alternative would be to have the teacher by your elbow calling out instructions.

We will take a look at flying techniques in Chapter 12, in the meantime let's get a glider for you to fly.

CHAPTER ELEVEN

A first radio control glider

Many people learn on a two channel model, rudder/elevator control being thought to be the minimum. There is no reason why you should not manage quite nicely with ailerons as well as or instead of rudder but since an aileron turn needs co-ordination of ailerons and elevator, rudder control is thought to be simpler.

You will have seen that for a servo to be able to operate a control surface, the rotary motion of the output arm needs to be converted into a straight line push. The link that is used clips into a hole on the arm and is free to pivot. This clips on and off the servo arm and is called a *quick link*. At the control surface end, there is a lever or *horn* which transfers the movement to the control surface. Between the two may be such as a wooden dowel or a wire within a tube and these are known as *pushrods* or *snakes*. Wire cables may run to a double lever such that it pulls one way and then pulls back the other. Since this needs to have no free play, it is known as a *closed* system. All these types of control are used on full-size gliders too and may use different types of screwed connections for adjustment. The amount of movement depends on the distances from the pivot point on the linkage. A matter of leverage and mechanical advantage again.

The type of model introduced here is a

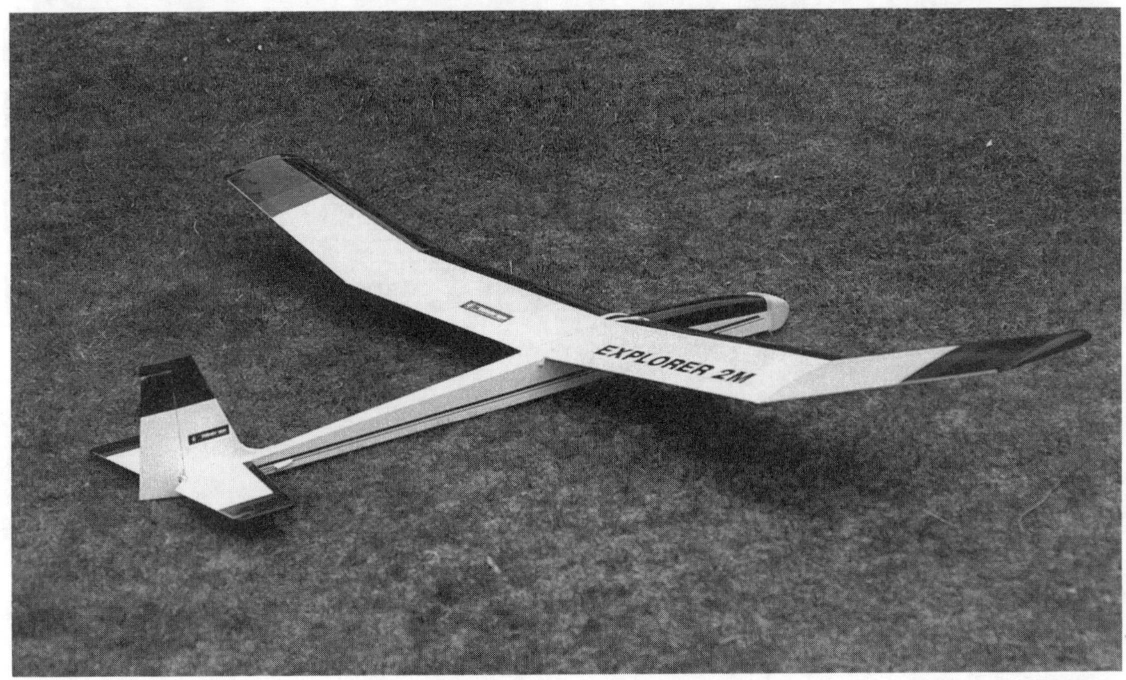

This glider is almost ready to fly. Rudder and elevator controls enough for starters.

simple rudder elevator device and you should have no problems in putting one together. Again, you may seek to buy a kit or even a ready-made model and some suitable ones are listed in the appendix. Things to watch for on setting up include a check on the structural integrity, sound joints with the wings and tail firm and not flopping about. The controls need to be moving in the right direction and to the right amount. Check the balance point and you should be ready for a test glide.

The trimming techniques are as with the free-flight glider with one subtle difference; with the radio control, changes can be made while the model is in flight. In fact not only trim changes but complete control over its flight.

Whether you fly it off a flat field or a slope depends largely on where you live and what facilities are available to you.

If you have made contact with a club, they will point you in the right direction and give you tuition. Otherwise, remember that all land belongs to someone somewhere so do not presume to trespass. Permission will often be given for long term use while being thrown off is usually for ever.
Let's get out into the open.

This training model has rudder elevator and aileron elevator versions. Grow with it.

CHAPTER TWELVE

Take to the skies

Here we will have a look at what you have to do to get the model into the air. For initial flat field flying, a useful piece of equipment to use is called a *bungee*. This uses a screw type dog stake, a section of rubber and a length of fishing line with a ring on the end laid downwind. A parachute is also a help since it will stretch tight when the glider is being launched, yet open up after release. The wind will then lay it neatly back by your feet ready for the next launch. The lengths generally in use are about 30 metres of rubber and 120 metres of line. A 50 pound breaking strain line should cover anything a beginner will be launching. You can use aerolastic chord but it is heavy and the cotton covering will restrict the stretch you can get. Of course,

if you join a club, you could probably use theirs.

So, you have checked that no one else is using your frequency, switched on, glide tested and happy?

Not too windy? If the wind is strong, best to stay at home and dream of your next project rather than risk it. Right, you have thought about that and there is a nice gentle drift.

Hook on and stretch the bungee. Not too far until you get the hang of things. A gentle nose up release has the model accelerating rapidly — while you correct with the rudder if it goes to one side or the other. As the rubber contracts, the model will slow down and perhaps a little down elevator may be necessary to release the

Eyes up the line as the pilot takes the strain of the stretched bungee.

line.

1st rule: don't take your eyes off it. Adjust the trim until the model has settled into a steady glide, then you can worry about steering it. Try left and right but do not hold the rudder on for as I warned earlier, the model will bank and rudder becomes down elevator. This rapidly becomes a spiral dive and a kersplat. To start with, use the 'dab, dab' technique which is a succession of quick control inputs followed by centralising the stick. Smart kids into calculus will know that a turn is actually a series of infinitely short straight lines. When the model is pointing in the right direction, stop moving the stick — but do be prepared to move it the other way as you will almost certainly have over controlled it.

This is quite normal because once a turn has been started, it will probably continue to try to turn. Remember about lag of inertia? Watch even an experienced car driver and you will doubtless see opposite steering needed to straighten up. Maybe you haven't thought about it but the first thing that you do when starting to turn on a bicycle is to move your handlebars the opposite way. This is the way to deflect it from its natural course and make it bank the way you want it to go. Try it but if you fall off, don't sue me.

2nd rule: down elevator gives control. If the glider is flying too slowly, it may be upset by a gust and the nose could rise. A quick dab of down elevator will keep air speed up and the model under control. As rudder is applied, the nose may in fact drop and it may be necessary to put in a little up elevator. You have the transmitter and will be responsible for watching the model and making any corrections that are necessary.

3rd rule: don't forget that the rudder is reversed when the glider is coming towards you. Still, an experienced pilot like you is not going to be caught out by that are you?

4th rule: when you are a beginner, avoid letting the model go downwind. Better to keep it flying up and down where you can see it. If you always make turns away from yourself, then there should be less opportunity for confusion with the rudder.

5th rule: always land into wind. For starters, any landing into wind which is in the same field is pretty good. You can weigh up the glide angle and with a bit of practice, you should soon be landing by your feet. When you can just bend down and switch off, you're getting good.

6th rule: if the model is going to land some distance away, maybe in long grass or shrubs, watch carefully where it goes. You can be within a few yards of a model and not know that it's there. Waggle the transmitter stick and you should hear the

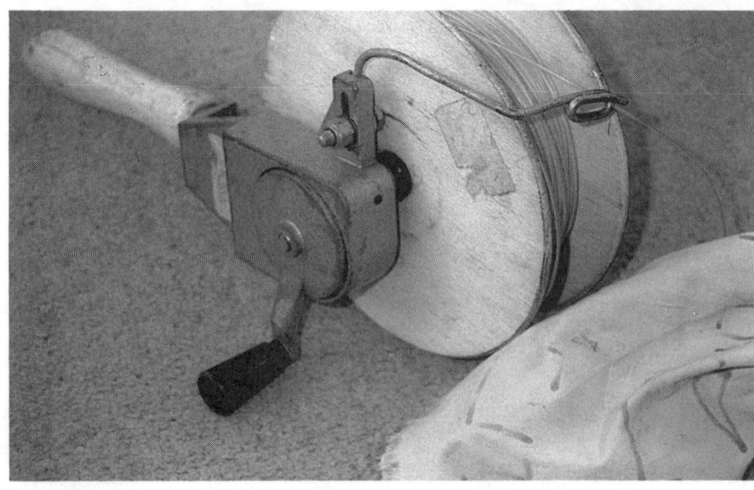

Grindstone gearbox makes a good basis for a tow line winch.

End of the line. A thermal soarer takes to the sky.

servos moving. There are lost model alarms available that sound when the transmitter is switched off or when the signal is lost. You should never need one if you do it right.

Enjoy that? Don't forget to switch off.

Practice makes perfect and when the left/right matter is sorted, you will be able to steer the model where you want it to be

and perhaps go to look for up going air.

Perhaps it's time we had a look at *slope soaring*. This could be called hill soaring or whatever else since anything from a sand dune, embankment or a mountain could provide the right conditions. In fact a sea-side site could be better than a mountain since the air is coming in smoothly off the sea and giving all the lift you could need. A mountain is likely to be difficult to get onto and if the lift is too good, it might be difficult to land. However, you must settle for what you can use and with a bit of imagination and an ordnance survey map, it should be possible to find somewhere suitable. Club members already flying slope soarers will give you an instant introduction however, and that is the preferred route. On the hill, a breeze is essential. No blow, no go. The wind should be blowing quite square onto the hill as well, along it or behind is no use. Slightly off is not too bad but for starters, let's make it easier.

A mass of air drifting across the area in

Even a low hill gives good lift. Here the Danish pilot is tacking up and down along the ridge.

front of the hill has only one course to take when it reaches the hill. Upwards. How fast it goes up depends upon the nature of the hill, some air may spill around the side, but it will be unstoppable. The air that you want to use is that which is going up and we will launch from somewhere near the top or where there is an edge. That is where the lift is.

Down the hill, the trees may be barely moving but at the top, it may be difficult to stand. The slope soarer's trick is to add lead ballast to make his glider fly faster, otherwise, it would be blown away. Where did you read that? Anyway, let's presume that there is a wind, it is square onto the hill and it is not too strong. You can be sure that any air coming towards you is going up and any glider or bird that is flying in that air will go up too.

The usual check, frequency clear, glider sound, switch on, controls working the right way and make ready to launch. Woah, have you checked the landing area and any downwind hazards? Yes? Good.

A smart throw, slightly downwards will get the model away but you will be surprised at the way that it suddenly goes up – bodily. Be prepared to throw in some rapid down elevator to increase the speed and penetrate forward away from the hill. That is where the smooth air is and that is where the best lift is. Well actually at an angle upwards and that is where we are going to fly. At this stage, you have two options; either turn or finish up having to make a long walk downhill and an even longer walk back up hill.

Let's turn.

Use the 'dab-dab' technique to get the model heading along to left or right with its nose just a little out from the slope. It could well continue on this heading until you decide to turn it again. The same trick gets the model drifting back the other way. Using this method, the glider is tacked up and down the ridge watching the altitude too. If the lift is good and the glider starts to get too high, apply down elevator trim

to keep within a few hundred yards. If down trim is applied, the glider will start to fly faster and be more responsive – that's good.

One benefit of slope soaring you will quickly notice is that with this lift, there is more 'stick time' between landings but sooner or later, land you must. Since we advocate that landings are made into wind, then at that stage, the model has to be flying towards you. That is indeed another advantage of slope soaring because when the turn is made towards you at each end of the ridge, it is possible to progressively drift back until the glider is level with you and actually flying towards you. Any confusion and the escape route out to lift and safety is obvious.

Get used to flying towards you and the final approach can be made by allowing the glider to drift downwind, then turn it back into wind and watch it settle down gracefully. Do not go too far back or there could be a long walk.

Why will it settle down behind the hill? As the air is rising up the front of the slope, it is being compressed and behind the hill, two things can happen. It will lose its speed gained as it was accelerated by the compression on the front and also, it will start to curl over in its own bit of turbulence. This part of the lift process is the opposite and is known as sink. Not quite the same as air following behind a thermal but just as effective in pulling a glider down. On the final approach, keep the airspeed on to maintain control authority through any turbulence or you might find the glider somewhere downwind. The trick is to be positive.

PARTY PIECE?

Slope soaring can be very entertaining too. From a bungee or a tow line on a flat field, the glider is going to start coming down. All the height you have or can make will be jealously conserved and the stop watch will be a measure of your success.

Fells like this are even better if you have one.

On the hill, on a good day there is a plentiful supply of lift and the problem may not be in keeping it up but in getting it down. Airbrakes may slow the model but one thing that you might have noticed is that feeding in down elevator makes the glider go faster since it is in a shallow dive. The better the lift, the steeper the effective dive and the faster it flies to stay in the same place.

Since you will know that energy can neither be created nor destroyed, we can only turn one form of energy into another. Let's say that a model is at a certain height above the ground. Its weight times its height is *potential energy*. Put the model into a dive and it is changed to *kinetic energy*. That is as a result of its speed (which is why a hammer has to be moving to drive a nail in). However, kinetic energy can be turned back into potential energy by zooming back up again. Maybe not as high because of air resistance or *drag*, though if the lift is that good, it might go even higher.

What this means is that there is more control of the model and since height can be turned into speed, there is the possibility of doing *aerobatics*. Maybe the rudder elevator model is a bit restricted but it will still do loops, stall turns, fly inverted, cuban eights and a few more advanced tricks. It is even possible to roll without ailerons.

So, we've had a look at flat field flying and slope soaring with a rudder and elevator model, what's that about ailerons?

CHAPTER THIRTEEN

Roll it over – and over

Aileron controls expand the aerobatic repertoire tremendously. Rudder and elevator work only in two dimensions and with dihedral, essential to steering control with a rudder only model, outside loops and manoeuvres including an outside element are going to be very difficult if not impossible.

I have described an aileron turn as rolling the model such that the elevator becomes a rudder. With ailerons however, it is possible to roll the aeroplane right over and back to upright again – time after time with the right method. It becomes a simple matter to roll the aeroplane to inverted and using a little down elevator, to keep the nose high and fly upside down as long as you may wish. You will remember that the rudder control appears to be reversed while the glider is flying towards you. What effect does flying inverted have on the aileron control? Looking at the model flying towards you, it may appear to be rolling the opposite way and this is quite understandable. However, the steering effect is unchanged. Go back to your first little test piece and you should see how this works. In fact inverted flying is quite easy, use the ailerons as if the model was the right way up but ease in a little down elevator to keep the nose up.

An aerobatic slope soarer typically has a

Full span ailerons mean that this model can be rolled, makes for three dimensional fun, rudder optional.

shorter span to help it roll faster. Manoeuvres generally involve an attempt to draw precise geometric patterns in the sky. Consider a loop however, which in a stiff wind has a number of elements not the least of which is the tendency to drift back down wind. Modern contests require the model to carry out aerobatics across the wind but even a loop into wind can be difficult. Let's start high up overhead and dive down to gain speed. When the model is at eye level heading straight and well out, pull the stick back gradually which puts the nose up into the beginning of the loop. Immediately, the wind lifts the aircraft trying to push it over faster. To counter this, the elevator must be slackened off. The top of the loop would be blown back needing more elevator while the dive down would tighten up and need to be opened up. Down elevator would be necessary to penetrate back to the start point. With the best will in the world, a loop into wind might appear from the side to be egg shaped. To loop across wind would be even more difficult and the rudder, where fitted, would be needed to prevent the model from getting blown back. The loop could be more concentric except that the slowing down on the up side has to balance the accelerating down side. Precise geometric shapes are not easy.

Consider the following top ten aerobatic manoeuvres for starters:

Continuous loops: the elevator has to be opened out on each downward pass to build up speed for the next one. These are likely to end as a series of ovals corkscrewing back into the hill.

Roll: dive for speed, pull the nose up and flip the aileron stick over. Practice tells you when to stop.

Continuous rolls: as before but be prepared to apply a little down elevator to keep the nose up while the model is inverted.

Stall turn: dive across wind and pull up, open to continue to climb and just before the model stalls, push across full rudder away from the slope such that the model dives back down the path it has just come up. With ailerons, this is also possible by momentarily pushing the aileron to turn away from the slope. The weathercock effect will flip the back end around. Continuous stall turns are great fun and very effective.

Roll off the top: half a loop with a pause while inverted at the top, followed by a half roll to upright.

Roll off the bottom: half an outside loop with a pause while inverted at the bottom followed by a half roll to upright.

Outside loop: dive from height to gain speed and go all the way round the loop finishing the right way up.

Cuban eight: three quarters of a loop followed by half a roll followed by another three quarters of a loop to finish.

Vertical eight: a full loop followed immediately by a dive into an outside loop finishing at the centre.

Horizontal eight: a loop followed immediately by an outside loop where each are at the same height.

There are lots of others but those will do for now. Remember that if you lose co-ordination at any time, that no matter what attitude the model is at, a dose of full up elevator will usually give you more time to get it out of trouble.

When you have more experience, do take more interest in aerobatics for their own sake — and yours. Because speed makes for improved control and the impetus of added ballast makes the model less likely to be deflected by wind drift, the result can be a fast flying package of adrenaline. You will know it when you have tried it.

CHAPTER FOURTEEN

Some modern methods and materials

Construction of these faster flying gliders has moved on somewhat since the slow flying, built up construction, free-flight glider was developed. Balsa and plywood fuselages are quite usual and tailplanes and rudders could well be carved from sheet balsa too. The biggest change though is in wing construction in which *expanded polystyrene foam* is cut to section using a *hot wire*. The wire is usually nickel chrome which has a high resistance and glows to a dull heat when carrying a current of up to a couple of amps. Pull this wire tight on a bow and it will cut through foam with great ease. Steer the wire by pinning templates onto the ends of the foam blocks and you have a very accurate core.

This core can be clad in wood veneer about one millimetre thick stuck on with *latex adhesive* (as used for sticking carpets) or epoxy resin. Often, these wings do not need a spar since the foam keeps the top and bottom skins apart, as with the spar test piece that you broke earlier. In fact, if a veneered foam wing fails as a result of a crash, it will show the same results in that the top skin will collapse inwards leaving the bottom skin possibly undamaged.

While white foam is most commonly used, foams with higher density have more compressive strength (resistance to collapsing inwards) and are used for more heavily loaded models. A blue foam commonly used in insulating buildings is

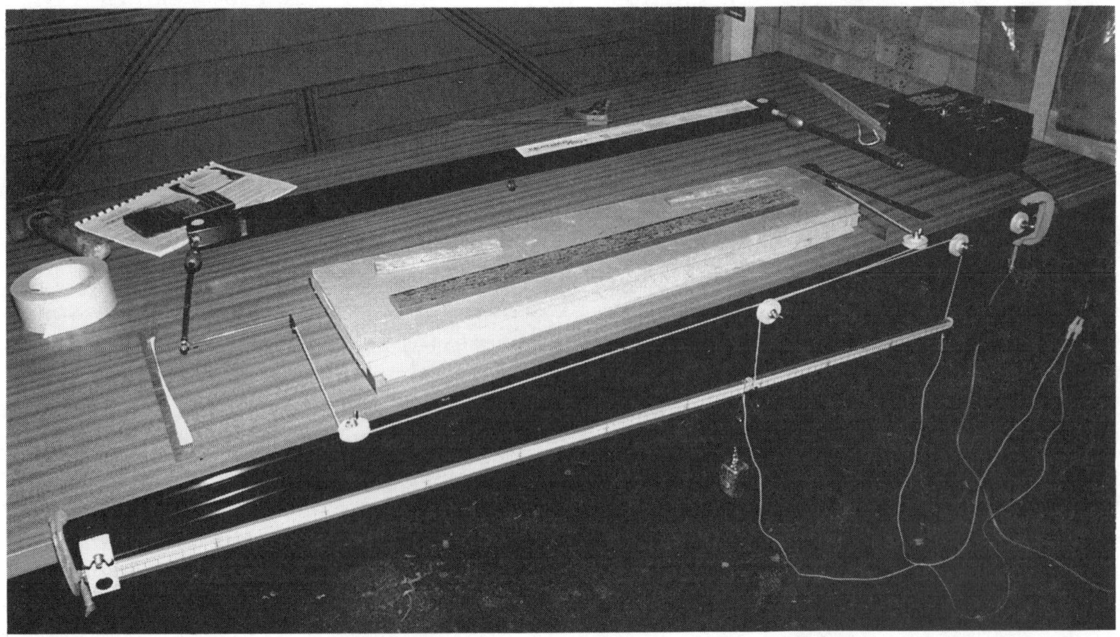

Foam wing cutting is not as complicated as it looks but easiest left to the specialists.

giving way to a pink variety which does not require CFCs in its manufacture, with ventilation, all cut well using the hot wire method and with spars moulded in, can be clad with glass cloth and epoxy.

There are different values of *epoxy resins* available, all flow and mix better when they are warmed and some low viscosity types are used for skinning wings with a lightweight fibre glass cloth. The result is a hard strong wing which is well worth the effort. Techniques have been developed in which the wing is covered in lightweight glass cloth, wetted out with epoxy resin and sealed in a plastic skin. This is sucked down onto the surface using a vacuum pump and results in a glass smooth surface which requires no sanding and which ensures that the resin is fully absorbed into the glass cloth.

Of the different resins available, *polyester resin* which is the material most widely used for what people know as fibre glass is not considered suitable for wing skinning. Being less expensive than epoxy, it is the resin most commonly used for moulded fuselages. With a densely pigmented gel coat, attractive mouldings can be reproduced quite quickly at moderate cost. Along with epoxy resins, we now have a wide range of reinforcing materials which are used in wing spars and fuselages. *Carbon fibre* and *kevlar* can be used as *tows* or multiple strands which when wetted out with resin form an immensely strong stucture. These materials do have different properties but both in tension and in shear are vastly superior to woven or chopped strand glass fibre. Complete spars are made from carbon fibre and this is the material widely used in building the elegant modern sailplane. Any place where glass reinforced plastic is used, you are likely to find these composites used as reinforcement. Shells of formula one racing cars, aircraft seats, you name it you'll find it. You may hear other names such as *Boron*, and *Dyneema* used in this context, don't worry about those yet, you have enough to learn about.

The most commonly used covering material these days is a heat shrink polyester *film* which has a coloured coating on one side. Low temperature such as with a domestic clothes iron is sufficient to soften the coating and stick it in place. A little more heat and it shrinks to a tight shiny surface and as there are a range of different films and colours available, it is possible to produce a distinctive and attractive model.

Adhesives have improved by leaps and bounds and almost anything can be stuck together or to anything else.

The traditional glue used to be balsa cement. This is a solution comprised of acetate dissolved in a suitable solvent such as acetone. Spread the glue, join the two parts together and as the solvent dries out, the two parts are stuck together. Once, that was the only option that we had. The most appropriate glue for balsa and ply now is *PVA* or poly vinyl acetate which has no smell, little taste and grabs quite quickly. The ordinary variety can be washed off clothing and it is quite safe for anyone to use. The problem is that if the model gets wet, the glue can soften and the model breaks up. Either keep it dry or use the waterproof variety which is also available. Hot melt glue is not so commonly used but two pack glue in which proportions are mixed together is. Epoxy resins are available which will set inside five minutes to give a workable joint or repair. It does take several hours at a moderate temperature to cure properly but it does work.

We cannot leave the section on modern materials without reference to cyanoacrylate. This adhesive is generally known as Superglue or *Cyano* in modelling circles. This adhesive was developed for field dressings in the war against North Vietnam to dispense with the need for stitching of wounds. Of course you all knew that. It does stick fingers together exceedingly well but it also gives off harmful vapours. In fact its use is now forbidden in certain industries. It has been used to tack together electronic components prior to soldering but application of heat causes it to give off a form of cyanide gas. It is possible to become sensitised to it, the effects are cumulative, possibly irreversible and in some people can cause the symptoms of asthma. This adhesive is powerful, it is ideal for field repairs but personally, my arms are not long enough to use it. You have been warned.

Probably as unpleasant can be the effects of the spray used as an *accelerator* for cyano. This is a derivative of trichlorethylene which is obnoxious at the best of times. Breathe in a mere few parts per million and you will know.

So it is with many of the materials that are available to us in the world today. Sanding glass fibre indoors can put a harmful dust into the lungs.

CHAPTER FIFTEEN

What about the weather?

There are those who talk about the 'flying season' and while I clearly understand the attractions of a warm sunny summer day with bees buzzing and birds chirping, do realise that gliding takes place all the year round. Of course, fog and rain will send anyone home early as it is not easy to fly a glider that you cannot see.

However, launching a glider up the line during one of those cold, clear frosty spells or standing in a cold wind, eyes streaming on top of a winter hill has to be experienced to be believed. The axiom has to be that if anyone can recognise you, then you are probably not wearing enough wind and waterproofs. Our weather forecasts are usually pretty good. Sometimes like horror-scopes (yes I know it's spelled wrongly but who believes that stuff anyway?) the wording is so vague that the forecast can be interpreted any way they choose. You know the form ''It will either rain or go dark before morning''... However, as a guide, the forecasts are not too bad and it should be possible to have either the calm weather thermal soarer or the ballasted slope soarer ready to take out.

The items to look for on a weather chart are the *Isobars* which join up points of equal pressure. Well spread out and the wind strengths are likely to be low but if the lines look like a thumb print, it is going to blow hard. Learn too about *fronts* which is where opposing masses of air at different temperatures and pressures meet. Air can be forced up or driven down, rapid cooling can dump vast quantities of rain water, or hail and snow, gales and squalls even and things would become generally unpleasant.

Don't let the threat keep you at home but do keep a weather eye upwind. It is possible to watch upwind and sense temperature changes which may signal the onset of rain. On the hill, one can usually see this falling well upwind and take the appropriate action.

Thermal generation is probably well enough understood but this does lead to a warning. Air adjacent to the ground will absorb radiated heat, especially over a heat source like a tarmac runway and will also absorb more moisture. This may break away and rise as a thermal and as it does so, it will expand and cool. As it cools, the moisture will condense out forming *cumulus clouds* (like the steam coming out of the kettle). Looking upwind, newly forming cumulus cloud will generally indicate the top of a thermal. Get under that. I mentioned that it is difficult to fly a glider when it cannot be seen. When warm moist air flowing towards a hill is deflected upwards, it is forced upwards with or without thermal activity and of course it will cool. As it cools, the moisture will condense out forming mist, known technically as *orographic cloud*. It is no use expecting it to blow past as it is forming all the time at the *dew point*, the temperature difference at which condensation takes place.

Information to pilots on an airport waveband radio will usually give temperature, pressure, dew point and wind strengths and these are updated regularly throughout the day. The wind strength where you are actually flying can be measured with the sort of device also used by yachtsmen in which air lifts a disc up a calibrated tapered tube. There are digital types and goodness knows what else but an experienced flyer will sense the wind strength and be quite accurate with his or her guesstimate.

There is a lot more to meteorology and its effect on soaring conditions and you have the delights of that to come. This book is after all about the basics.

CHAPTER SIXTEEN

Where to next?

You may decide that you would like to get involved with full-size gliding and there are plenty of clubs that offer residential courses. There you will find that many of the pilots have a great interest in radio control model gliding. So what keeps their interest? The answer probably is variety. The range of activities and interests covered is tremendous and there is no reason why anyone should ever tire of radio gliding.

On the flat field, the challenge is invariably to use up going air to prolong the flight and this can be sufficient challenge in itself. Contests are organised where the challenge is to keep it up for the maximum time in a given working period. There may be penalties for over flying the allowed time and bonuses are given for landing within a circle in some types of events. These contests may be in various categories including:

Hand launched gliders generally up to 60" span and which weigh around ten to fifteen ounces. An ace javelin thrower may launch one of these to a good height though contests tend to use a short bungee in order to equalise young and old.

Two metre maximum span, rudder elevator only. This tends to be an informal class and may permit the use of a bungee launch or a hand tow. The maximum flight time for the day may be set at say five minutes, perhaps five attempts with the worse score to be discarded. There would be no penalty for over flying. One international variation on this theme is consecutive flights of two to seven minutes with points lost for landing outside the time but a bonus to be gained for a neat landing astride a tape.

Two metre models can be as simple as you like. This lightweight has a V-tail.

This 'chuckie' weighs less than eight ounces and soars happily off low buildings.

Pit scene has a couple of 100'' class models keeping close company.

100 inch span, rudder and elevator plus optional airbrakes. Launch from a hand tow using a line of 150 metres in length. This line is wound on to a drum after the model has been released and flight times are nominated.

This open class model is 4m span.

50

Open class. No limit on span and the model may have ailerons, airbrakes and flaps. Hand tow would be used as in 100″. This is also flown as an international class to slightly more complicated rules which may permit the use of hand tow or bungee.

International multi task. Each round is flown with separate flights to record maximum speed over four laps of a 150 metre course, the maximum number of laps in a given time and a precision flight where models have to land on a given spot in a precise time. These models are launched from an electric powered winch and the heights achieved are awesome as are the speeds. 600 metres in 16 seconds or so works out at an average speed of over 80 mph, that includes the turns — and with a glider too.

At the other extreme, there still exists a great following for *vintage* designs, many of which are sixty or more years old.

There are also categories for gliders powered by *electric motors*. The performance is measured with the motor switched off so the motor is really the means to get the model into the air. That may sound gentle but some of these models have very powerful motors, they can be heavy when laden with batteries and they really go. Of course, there are sedate sport electric models too, you takes your choice.

Hill soaring events are very popular and cover as wide a range of interests. Closer to the efforts of the flat field, thermal soaring fraternity is the type of event known as *slope cross country*. In fact this is an attempt to reach a number of gates which are marked by a flag and post and carry out various tasks with the glider that you are flying. This may involve a simple turn overhead — passing back over the gate, turning back into wind, making a full turn and then out again to complete the task. The ability to recognise lift, whether slope or thermal generated is important and this can combine the elements of the two disciplines. Every few gates, there may be a low pass task where the glider has to

International multi task models are high tech and use electric winches for launching.

This vintage design is from 1949. Vintage models are always popular.

Competitors get away on another cross country flight. Good exercise, challenging flying.

be flown below the horizon in order to shed height and make the next task even more difficult. This is easy enough when the gates are on the front of the hill but harder when they are located in the area of sink further back.

Power scale soaring or PSS is an increasingly popular class which has the modeller producing a gliding model of any aircraft originally powered by piston, rocket or jet engines.

Many beaver away researching rare prototypes in order to come up with something different, but others are quite happy to turn up with a well known aircraft which performs in a very creditable manner. Subjects chosen have ranged from small lightweight aircraft right up to giant bombers and jumbo jets. Working details can include lights, machine gun noise, retracting undercarriages, parachute drops or anything else that you can imagine. Models are judged on accuracy of outline, colour scheme and finish – your imagination is the only restriction.

Slope soaring also lends itself to gliding models of birds and the choice of subjects is very wide. From swifts up to condors with sea birds and eagles in between have been chosen and with an illusory paint scheme, can even fool other birds. The *FSS* category of gliding models of creatures originally covered by feathers, scales or skin has even produced models of pterodactyls,

Slope racing may have one model at a time against a stop watch timed over ten laps of a 100 metre course. These models are very efficient and super fast with the turn technique needing anticipation to cut down wasted time. The machines frequently use all moulded glass reinforced plastics in their construction with computerised transmitters to offer more control.

At a simpler level, *pylon racing* using models no bigger than 60 inches wing span are a lot of fun. There may be four models on the course at a time with flag men and helpers and mid-air collisions are not unknown. Exciting though...

Scale gliders are also well supported internationally. Modern sailplanes are mostly of moulded GRP construction and are, without exception, elegant creations. You may aspire to fly one of these some

These are gliders. Full size aircraft make good choices for slope soaring.

This fully aerobatic gull fools the real cliff dwellers. They can't loop or roll.

Pylon racing one against the clock or four up gets the adrenaline going. Try it some day.

day and who knows? There are plenty of kits about to choose from for the modern machines but there are also plans to build from too. Although modern craft have a special appeal, it must be remembered that gliding has been around for many years, in fact the first ever flights were in a glider as mentioned earlier. People have pursued the search for excellence and improvement in performance ever since and many really delightful gliders have been produced all around the world. This was particularly true of Germany where they were forbidden to have an airforce after World War 1. In developing a range of high performance gliders and training literally thousands of young men to fly them, they were able to rapidly establish a devastating air force before World War 2. Crafty, hm? Nevertheless, vintage gliders and those produced prior to the introduction of GRP lend themselves better to traditional modelling methods and materials and hold

Scale gliders both modern and vintage are very satisfying to fly. This Minimoa is typical of mid thirties German developments.

a deservedly popular place in scale model gliding.

The description *hobby* is especially suited to the production of both *vintage, post vintage* and *glass* scale glider models. Many enthusiasts take a pride in their workmanship and a photograph might fool anyone but the cameraman. Museum-piece might be an apt description except that these people take them out and fly them. I should mention that scale gliders are flown from the flat launching by winch or aerotow too and adds yet another facet to this fascinating sport.

The final example is that of *aerobatics* which I mentioned earlier. A schedule may be set in which a set series of *manoeuvres* is to be carried out in a limited time. One or maybe two pilots are flying at any one time so the contest is likely to drag a bit while awaiting your turn.

It is a good opportunity to watch other flyers perform, there is much to learn. All of the selected aerobatics require speed, speed needs height to start with and the schedule will not allow the contestant to wait for a thermal. Poor flying with excess-ive control inputs create drag which will cost height and therefore time. Smooth flying to carefully conserve energy is the secret here but why just in aerobatics. Any skills needed for this type of display will certainly improve your performance in any other class and really, this type of flying is the key to success and satisfaction.

Many glider flyers take a delight in showing off their proficiency, their models and their flying skill with never a thought to contests and it shows.

Proficiency is a word that you will come to recognise since a number of clubs operate an *Achievement Scheme* or prog-ressive teaching schedule and there are different grades to aim for. Some of the programmes have been set by national bodies and your club mates will organise a teach-in to take you through the various stages as you proceed. The tests are voluntary but you would be well advised to take it seriously. Heaven forbid that you should be hit by a model being flown by an incompetent pilot. We all need to continually upgrade our standards.

CHAPTER SEVENTEEN

How do we start?

The important thing to do before you commit yourself to time and money is to make a visit to your local clubs and see what is going on there. Visit both full size and modelling clubs, they have all got a lot going for them and consider too that it doesn't really matter what you do, as long as you do something.

The British Gliding Association also have many clubs and an intelligent approach from a serious enquirer will get you the full conducted tour. Don't expect a sample flight for free — they still have to pay the insurance but you will get a good reception. That is unless you go on a superb day when club members are queuing up to get onto the site. They always have first call on any aircraft unless there is a recognised course taking place. The courses are usually over five days, Monday to Friday and a gliding holiday is always good value for money.

There are well over five hundred aeromodelling clubs in the UK and most of these have an active gliding section. Make contact and armed with this book, at least you won't be too much in the dark when you start to talk to the members. Don't expect them to come and talk to you, they have enough on their minds but choose your moment, ask a question and you will be surprised how helpful they can be. The times not to talk to a modeller are when he is getting ready to launch, during his flight and when the model is on final approach. Apart from that, you will find the flyer quite amiable — unless of course he has had a hard landing.

Among your questions, you might ask if anyone has a second hand model to sell. It is possible that you could pick up something serviceable for a modest sum. It may look a bit tatty but it has probably had the weak

"Gliding is child's play", says this young 'un, but he has a lot to learn.

spots repaired out of it and all the flying bugs too. Ask nicely and you might even get some tuition too. It is also possible that when you have learned on this trainer, that you might be able to sell it on and the exercise will not have cost a fortune. Talk to as many people as possible and find out what sort of gliding activities are popular with them. Do not think about a slope soarer if they are only interested in flat field soaring though one in the car boot on holiday is always a good bet. However, most clubs do both flat field and slope soaring and probably electric flight too. Keep your eyes and ears open and you will rapidly enjoy the company of a new circle of friends. Don't think because you have read this book from cover to cover that you now know all the answers. I certainly don't.

Sources of information

Find a model club by contacting the *British Model Flying Association*. This is the body delegated by the Civil Aviation Authority and the Federation Aeronautique Internationale to take care of aeromodelling interests in Britain. They have a comprehensive insurance scheme and a bi-monthly magazine in newspaper format. Their members also run contests of all categories to international and national rules and have an achievement scheme.

BMFA, 31 St Andrews Road, Leicester, LE2 8RE, phone 01533 440028, fax 01533 440465.

If you are interested in thermal soaring competitions, then the *British Association of Radio Control Soarers* could be a useful contact. They run events for flat field and slope and publish an interesting magazine quarterly. BARCS have an insurance scheme and their achievement schemes for glider and electric have largely been adopted by the BMFA.

BARCS, Brian Pettit, 36 Windmill Avenue, Wokingham, Berks, RG11 2XD. 01734 783824.

Your *local hobby shop*, which you could well find in the *Yellow Pages* will introduce you to a local club or like minded individuals. Check that the proprietor is prepared to give you some help and advice if need be. There are those who might sell you something unsuitable to make a sale but mostly, they are a great bunch who will do what they can to help.

Mail order is a good way of buying equipment but you will still need someone to be there when you want them. I suggest that you do not buy your gear at the discount shop and take it the shop round the corner to have it serviced...

The Model Pilots' Association is organised by Nexus Special Interests, who publish various model aircraft magazines including *Silent Flight, Aeromodeller, Radio Control Models and Electronics, Radio Modeller* and *Scale Aircraft*.. They also have an insurance scheme which caters for all modelling interests. *Silent Flight* is the only magazine which caters exclusively for gliding and electric powered soarers.

Model Pilots Association, Nexus Special Interests Ltd., Nexus House, Boundary Way, Hemel Hempstead, Herts, HP2 7ST, phone 01442 66551, fax 01442 66998.

The *British Gliding Association* will introduce you to a suitable full size gliding club. Write direct to obtain gliding holidays, tuition and membership details. There are occasionally discounts to course members who join on completion of a gliding course — or maybe even before. Check. The BGA will send you a rather nicely produced leaflet explaining what you are letting yourself in for. Most helpful.

British Gliding Association, Kimberley House, Vaughan Way, Leicester, LE1 4SE. 01162 531051

RECOMMENDED READING

Thermal Soaring by George Stringwell (R.M. Books). A very experienced modeller and long time magazine contributor. This book details building and flying techniques and has to be the best of the bunch.

Flying Scale Gliders by Chas Gardiner. (Nexus Special Interests) The full background and lots of useful stuff on scale model gliders and Power Scale Soarers.

Radio Control Soaring by Dave Hughes. (Radio Control Publishing Co. Ltd) This was the first handbook for the radio gliding enthusiast written by a pioneer in model aircraft magazine publication.

Radio Control Slope Soaring by Dave Hughes. (R M Books Ltd.) Much of the slope material from the earlier book updated.

Radio Control Foam Modelling by David Thomas. (Nexus Special Interests) Lots of helpful stuff on building models from foam. Things have moved on a bit but most of the stuff you will need to know to start with is there

Model Aircraft Plans Handbook. (Nexus Special Interests) Nexus have the biggest and best range of plans (probably) in the world from free flight, control line and vintage right through to RC scale. There are informative sections on construction etc and the cost of the book is £2.95 — recoverable on the first order.

Model Aircraft Aerodynamics by Martin Simons. (Nexus Special Interests) Now in its third edition, this is the definitive book on model aircraft technicalities and should be required reading for aeronautical students.

Meteorology for Glider Pilots by C E Wallington. (J. W. Arrowsmith) Aimed mainly at the pilots of full size gliders, this book nevertheless makes good reading and helps the reader understand the factors influencing weather for soarers.

Some suitable models to start with

Free-flight trimming; Although there are a number of small ready made chuck gliders available at various retail outlets, you will learn more by constructing the example given. In addition to the built up towline glider described, a suitable kit is the West Wings Merlin available from most model aircraft retailers.

Suitable free flight designs from the Plans Handbook include:

Golden Wings, 44'' span. Simple and sure flier. (Vic Smeed, G594).

May Morning . 36'' span. Designed especially for beginners. (Andy Crisp, G1253).

Also from the Plans Handbook, suitable early rudder and elevator radio control models include:

Soarcerer, 52'' span. Drawing shows aileron conversion. (Dave Hughes, RM47).

Unique Monique. 72'' span with simple construction. (Joe Dibble, RM98).

Morphix, this two metre model has alternative wings for thermal and slope aerobatics. (Chas Gardiner, RC1596).

An excellent and inexpensive lightweight thermal soarer kit is the Sonata. by the Balsa Cabin. Almost ready to fly (ARTF) models are available including such as the Explorer two metre model. There are others — your clubmates or model shop will advise.

Kits recommended include the Ace from Soar Ahead Sailplanes, The Fledgling from Flair Products and the Middlephase from Chris Foss Designs. These also lead to aileron models. If a model is not listed here, it does not mean that it is unsuitable. If in doubt, ask.